HOW TO WRITE PULP FICTION

JAMES SCOTT BELL

Published by Compendium Press

CONTENTS

WHAT IS PULP FICTION?

There was a desert wind blowing that night. It was one of those hot dry Santa Anas that come down through the mountain passes and curl your hair and make your nerves jump and your skin itch. On nights like that every booze party ends in a fight. Meek little wives feel the edge of the carving knife and study their husbands' necks.

That's the opening of the classic pulp story "Red Wind" by one of the greatest practitioners of the form, Raymond Chandler. The paragraph sets a tone. It gives you a sense of what's coming. We know it'll have at least one dead body and plenty of sharp gab.

Pulp doesn't bog us down with thematic ambiguity or thick flights of circumlocutory style. (I consulted a thesaurus to get *circumlocutory*, which is exactly the kind of thing pulp doesn't do.)

Pulp is escapist and entertaining.

And there's absolutely nothing wrong with that.

In fact, there's a lot that's right with it. At its best, pulp fiction provides a product that is every bit as desirable as a grilled hamburger made from choice ground beef, on a fresh bun, and all the right fixin's. More hamburgers, by far, are consumed in this land than prime rib or filet. And when the joint that serves them up makes a quality munch every time, it engenders lots of repeat business.

So it is with quality pulp. It's a fair exchange of money for diversion.

In the classic pulp era, roughly 1910–1950, many a scribe who could deliver the goods made enough dough for food and drink and a roof ... and sometimes even a family. They knew what the market wanted and how to shape stories for the various genres.

And just as the fundamentals of a good hamburger have not changed, the basics of putting together a good pulp story remain constant. It's the spice that you add that makes yours unique.

What has changed, of course, is the delivery system for books and stories.

The Kindle changed everything. For the good of both writers and readers.

Now we read on smart phones and tablets, and listen to audio.

All of which, for the writer who wants to make some lettuce at this game, spells opportunity.

JUST WHAT IS PULP FICTION?

The term *pulp fiction* has a rich history and multifaceted meanings.

To some, pulp is fiction that provides transient pleasure, and nothing else.

To others, it's hack work, "low quality," a threat to literature itself!

Bosh to both extremes.

Some of the best prose stylists in American lit—such as Raymond Chandler and John D. MacDonald—were trained and nurtured by the pulps.

Historically, pulp fiction was that which was printed on cheap, wood-pulp paper and set inside lurid, colorful covers of magazines selling for a dime or fifteen cents. America in the 1920s and 30s was voracious in its reading habits, consuming not just books but an ocean of stories provided in well over a hundred magazines. The most famous pulps included *Black Mask, Weird Tales, Dime Detective, Amazing Stories, Argosy,* and *Adventure.* The most popular genres were detective, mystery, adventure, Westerns, confessionals, and fantasy.

Readers could not get enough of series characters like Perry Mason (by Erle Stanley Gardner); Tarzan (Edgar Rice Burroughs); Doc Savage (Lester Dent); and The Shadow (Walter B. Gibson).

The ladies were represented as well. A series featuring college-educated Ellen Patrick, who fought corruption in 30s Los Angeles as "the Domino Lady," appeared in the pulp magazine *Saucy Romantic Adventures.* (Now wouldn't you like to have a few original copies of that?)

Then the pulp writer's world expanded with the onset of mass market paperbacks.

The first paperback publisher, Pocket Books, was established in 1939. It was followed by several other firms, including Avon and Dell. The books they produced sold for a quarter or less and were sized to fit on wire-rack "spinners." That's because traditional bookstores—much fewer in number before the chains arose in the 1960s—concentrated on hardcovers. The paperback companies saw a huge market waiting for them at newsstands, train stations, lunch counters, the corner cigar store, and virtually any other place with consumer traffic.

Using enticing covers, they banked on impulse buys. For a mere twenty-five cents, a businessman going on the road could pick up a reprint of a classic or maybe a good murder mystery. A housewife could snatch up a book along with her groceries.

World War II changed the market forever. Returning GIs weren't into classics or cozy mysteries or romances. So the hard-boiled school of paperbacks sprang up, starting with Mickey

Spillane's *I, the Jury* in 1947. The era of fast-paced crime stories with salacious covers had begun.

The 1950s saw an explosion of noir-ish fiction by authors such as John D. MacDonald, Jim Thompson, and David Goodis. Science fiction came barreling in, too, with prolific writers like Robert A. Heinlein and Isaac Asimov.

In the 60s, series characters proved enduringly popular. Shell Scott (by Richard Prather); Travis McGee (John D. MacDonald); and Mack Bolan (Don Pendleton) sold in the millions.

The 1970s brought the biggest pulp genre of all—category romance—to the fore.

In the 1980s, women began to enter the hardboiled market. Like Sarah Paretsky and her series character V. I. Warshawski: and Sue Grafton with Kinsey Millhone.

By the time the 90s rolled around, paperback fiction covered all genres, and was wide and deep with talent.

But then something happened. Something that has killed the mass-market paperback.

A little something called The Kindle.

Suddenly, with less expensive (and often free) pulp available online, and with bookstore chains closing (Borders) or shrinking (Barnes & Noble) the shelf space for mass-market all but disappeared.

In its place now is the new pulp of original, digital content.

With all that to look back on, we can make some generalizations about the breadth and style of pulp. In general, pulp fiction is:

- Plot-centric
- Easy to read (no need to run to the dictionary)
- Fast-paced

Pulp fiction is enhanced by:

- Colorful characters
- Snappy dialogue
- Intriguing settings

At its best, pulp fiction is *satisfying*. It meets a need, a legit one —the need for temporary respite from everyday life. That's what readers of pulp have always desired.

That being said, what is it that the pulp writer desires?

It's pretty basic and, once again, perfectly legitimate.

WHAT A PULP WRITER WANTS

The philosophy of the pulp writer is to make money by writing fiction. He is not ashamed of this, for it is nothing to be ashamed of. Writing is a commercial transaction under the free enterprise system. The pulp writer provides a product and wants as many people to buy the product as possible.

The successful pulpster knows there is a *craft* to storytelling which must be learned and practiced. Even more, he knows one of

é11111111ae1aé1

the keys to success is being prolific. Words must be produced with a certain amount of regularity, if not outright speed.

The pulp writer can coexist with the literary writer, but often the latter picks a fight.

Like this one (who shall remain nameless) who wrote the following:

> All writers wish for commercial success. But at what price? If you sell your soul to the devil of profitability, you have to be able to look in the mirror every day and say, without flinching, that you're a commercial writer.

The pulp writer responds, "I look at myself in the mirror every morning, and I like what I see. Selling my soul to the devil? Excuse me? Is a plumber who prides himself on a job well done and who gets paid selling himself to the devil? Or the writer who wants to provide what so many readers want—a dream, a distraction, some joy? Gimme a break!"

A successful pulp writer named William Wallace Cook (writing under the pen name John Milton Edwards) wrote this over 100 years ago:

> The tale that moves breathlessly but logically, that is built incident upon incident to a telling climax with the frankly avowed purpose to entertain, that has no questionable leanings or immoral affiliations—such a tale speeds innocently an idle hour, diverts pleasantly the harassed mind, freshens our zeal for the duties of life, and occasionally leaves us with higher ideals.
>
> We are all dreamers. We must be dreamers before we are doers. If some of the visions that come to us in secret reverie were flaunted in all their conceit and inconsistency before the world, not one of us but would be the butt of the world's ridicule. And yet, out of these highly tinted imaginings springs the impulse that carries us to higher and nobler things.

A difference in the price of two commodities does not necessarily mark a moral difference in the commodities themselves. *The Century Magazine* sells for 35 cents, while *The Argosy* sells for 10 cents. You will be told that *The Century* is "high class" and with a distinct literary flavor, perhaps that it is more elevating. Even so; yet which of these magazines is doing more to make the world really livable? Ask the newsdealer in your town how many *Centuries* he sells, and how many *Argosies*.

Readers are not made for the popular magazines, but the popular magazines are made for the people. Unless there was a distinct and insistent demand for this sort of entertainment, so many all-story magazines, priced at a dime, could not exist. (Cook/Edwards, *The Fiction Factory*, 1912, The Editor Company)

Pulp writers are secure in knowing that they help make "the world really livable" by providing the dream-like experience of a solid, entertaining story. When the National Book Award nominates five novels that sold an average of 4,000 copies each, the pulp writer is not angry or envious. He is fine with the fact that such novels are produced. On occasion, he reads one. (Though when he does, you may hear him muttering *Do something already!*)

The successful pulp writer knows it is good to make dough, provide entertainment, and be known as a solid craftsman.

And knows, too, that the writing game is a battle. Now, more than ever, it's a battle for attention.

TYPE HARD, TYPE FAST

It's the distractions, sweetie.

No, that's not a line of dialogue from a pulp private-eye story. It's the reality of our time. We are awash in an exploding universe of stimuli, screaming for our attention.

As one book industry insider put it, the internet "is in a trillion-dollars arms race" to grab and keep you. Even if they break through the noise and get someone's attention, there is an ongoing battle to keep that person interested in more of your product.

So the challenge is not just to find readers, but to induce them to buy more of your fiction as soon as it's available.

A report in *The Economist* (Feb. 9, 2017) put it this way:

> The entertainment business is a never-ending and ever-intensifying war for consumers' limited time and attention. Around the clock, each minute is contested by companies like Facebook, Instagram, Google, YouTube, Snap, Amazon, Disney, Comcast, AT&T, Sky, Fox and Netflix. Consumers can take in only so much of what is on offer. As this report has shown, faced with an overwhelming array of choices and guided by menus, digital rankings and suggestions calculated by algorithms, they

increasingly pick from just a few of the most popular items. Technology and media companies are doing their utmost to induce users to spend even more time on each of their platforms every day. From tweaking algorithms to stepping up notifications to endlessly scrolling feeds, technology has turned human distraction into its metric of profit.

That's why, for the pulp fiction writer, content is king. Getting more of the product out there. They type hard and type fast.

TYPE HARD

Type hard refers to the mindset of the pulpster. It's an attitude that says, *I'm charging ahead. I don't care about the obstacles. I don't give a rip about the odds. I haven't got the time or the interest to think about the "cant's." Writing is what I do, so I do it.*

This is how pulp writers had to think during the Great Depression.

Imagine getting fired from a job and not being able to find another. You need to put food on the table. There's a big pulp market out there, so you hock what you need to in order to buy a typewriter and move to New York. You give yourself six months to get published. You type your stories in a cold-water flat and make the rounds of the publishing offices every day.

That was a common theme in the 1930s. One such writer was Frank Gruber, who wrote about his experiences in a wonderful memoir, *The Pulp Jungle*. In July of 1934, Gruber moved to New York with a plan to get published within six months.

My physical assets consisted of one portable Remington typewriter and my wardrobe which, aside from what I was wearing, fit very comfortably into one medium size suitcase. I had sixty dollars in cash, but paid out ten dollars and fifty cents of it for a week's rent in advance at the Forty-fourth Street Hotel. I squandered another ten dollars over the long weekend, so that on Tuesday morning, when I went out to size up the pulp jungle I had approximately forty dollars.

I had one thing else ... the will to succeed.

That's what typing hard means. The iron will to succeed. Have you got it?

That's the first requirement of the pulp writer.

TYPE FAST

The other thing these writers did was type *a whole lot of words*.

Some of them—like Erle Stanley Gardner and W. T. Ballard—averaged a million words a year. A million!

That's the equivalent of *fifteen full-length novels every single year!*

Frank Gruber tells about a writer named George Bruce who used to throw parties in his small Brooklyn apartment. One night the place was jammed with thirty-plus people. At ten o'clock Bruce announced he had a 12,000-word story due the following morning. He went to a corner where his typewriter was and pounded it for four hours, ignoring the party swirling around him. At two o'clock in the morning he announced he was finished and poured himself a glass of gin.

Gruber also got to know the most prolific author of all time. His name was Frederick Faust, but you know him by his famous pen name, Max Brand. When Gruber met him, they were in Hollywood working at Warner Bros. Studios. Faust had, by that time, written and published approximately forty-five million words.

Gruber asked Faust how on earth he did it. Faust asked Gruber if he could write fourteen pages in one day. Gruber said he'd certainly done so (fourteen pages is about 4,000 words), but had also gone two or three weeks without writing a line.

That was the secret, Faust said. He wrote fourteen pages a day, every day, "come rain or shine, come mood or no."

That works out to one and a half million words a year.

The really remarkable thing about Fred Faust's output was that he was the "biggest drinker" Gruber ever met. Faust would put away a thermos of whiskey during his morning writing hours. His lunch would be washed down by several more drinks. "When he went home at five-thirty," Gruber writes, "he had a light supper and then settled down to his serious drinking."

Faust was one of those extremely rare individuals who could drink like that every night and still operate in the morning. *I do not recommend this method.*

I do, however, recommend Faust's seriousness about a quota. I'm a piker compared to guys like Faust and Erle Stanley Gardner, but I can tell you my average yearly output for the last seventeen years: a little north of 300,000 words. I keep track on a spreadsheet. It's the most important writing practice I know. It's the only way I've been able to write over fifty books, several novellas, a memoir, and many short stories—most of them published and making it possible for me to make my living as a writer.

Now, I know most of you do not have the luxury of quitting your day job and moving to New York. Or Yonkers. Or any other place.

You have family and a day job and obligations in your home town.

You want to write, but you have to squeeze in the time and can't get all that much done.

That's all right. The pulp authors of old would welcome you into the club if you have an iron determination and fulfill *whatever quota you are capable of.*

Take a look at your weekly schedule. Figure out the times you can dedicate to your writing. Cut something out if you have to, to get a little bit more. Do you really need to watch that *Seinfeld* episode you've seen twenty times? Is all that social media time really necessary?

Take a couple of weeks where you write as many words as you comfortably can. See what that weekly quota works out to.

Get used to writing without your "inner editor" blocking you. A pulp writer writes freely when at the keyboard.

Whatever your comfortable weekly quota is, up that by 10%. True pulp writers must feel at least a little bit of pressure.

Keep track of the words you produce in a week. Optimally, you write something every day. (I divide my weekly 6,000-word quota into six days. If I miss a day for some reason, I make up for it on the other days. And I take one day off a week. This recharges my batteries, which is necessary for the pulp writer!)

Just keep typing. And don't complain about the odds. Your pulp forebears wouldn't like that. They'd have a message for you.

•You don't know how good you've got it compared to our day! You can publish yourself, to a virtually unlimited market! Man, what we wouldn't have given for that!

•If you don't write to a quota, I have no sympathy for you.

•If you don't pay at least some attention to the market, I think you're daft.

•If you don't try to get better at your craft, you'd be better off as a plumber, and the sooner the better.

•If you want to make it, keep working. And the work never stops!

Are you willing to sign on as a pulp writer?

Good.

Let's set up some conditions for success.

CONDITIONS FOR SUCCESS

Ray Bradbury once said, "You must stay drunk on writing so reality cannot destroy you."

There's a certain poetic truth in that for the pulp writer. The writing itself must be a sort of intoxicant. Because, when it is, it shows up on the page.

Cook/Edwards, in *The Fiction Factory*, put it this way:

The sentiment which Edwards has tried to carry through every paragraph and line of this book is this, that "Writing is its own reward." His meaning is, that to the writer the joy of the work is something infinitely higher, finer and more satisfying than its pecuniary value to the editor who buys it. Material success, of course, is a necessity, unless – happy condition! – the writer has a private income on which to draw for meeting the sordid demands of life. But this also is true: A writer even of modest talent will have material success in a direct ratio with the joy he finds in his work! – Because, brother of the pen, when one takes pleasure in an effort, then that effort attracts merit inevitably. If any writing is a merciless grind the result will show it – and the editor will see it, and reject.

This joy is the necessary antidote to doubt.

All writers deal with doubt. They wonder if they're good enough, if all the effort will ever "pay off." For which Cook/Edwards also had advice:

There are times, however, when doubt shakes the firmest confidence. A writer will have moods into which will creep a distrust of the work upon which he is at that moment engaged. If necessity spurs him on and he cannot rise above his misgivings, the story will testify to the lack of faith, doubts will increase as defects multiply and the story will be ruined. THE WRITER MUST HAVE FAITH IN HIS WORK QUITE APART FROM THE MONEY HE EXPECTS TO RECEIVE FOR IT. If he has this faith he reaches toward a spiritual success beside which the highest material success is paltry indeed.

When a writer sits down to a story let him blind his eyes to the financial returns, even though they may be sorely needed. Let him forget that his wares are to be offered for sale, and consider them as being wrought for his own diversion. Let him say to himself, "I shall make this the best story I have ever written; I shall weave my soul into its warp and whether it sells or not I shall be satisfied to know that I have put upon paper the BEST that is in me." If he will do this, he will achieve a spiritual success and – as surely as day follows night – a material success beyond his fondest dreams. BUT he must keep his eye single to the TRUE success and must have no commerce in thought with what may come to him materially.

So making writing its own reward is the first condition of pulp writing success.

HEALTH

It goes without saying that the healthier your body and mind, the better your production will be. The history of pulp fiction—indeed, of writing in general—is littered with the remains of writers whose output suffered due to booze, chain smoking, or dietary overindulgence. I'm not going to give you a master plan for your personal health. You can get that on your own. I simply mention it here as a reminder to take care of your precious brain.

CRAFT STUDY

Alongside your output of words, determine to constantly improve your knowledge of the fiction craft.

There are abundant resources available to you in books, blogs, and *Writer's Digest* magazine. All of the craft of fiction writing can be placed under one of what I call the seven critical success factors: plot, structure, characters, scenes, dialogue, voice, and theme. You can go over each area with a trusted advisor and see which ones need the most improvement. Prioritize the areas, with your weakest first, then put together a self-study plan for improvement in each one.

BETA READERS AND EDITORS

Feedback on works-in-progress is essential. Some of it's free (beta readers) and some you pay for (freelance editors).

BETA READERS

Beta readers are those folks who are willing to give you a helping hand without compensation (though I will sometimes send a gift card or some such). These should not be close relatives, because you want honesty and no drama. With a little bit of effort, you'll be able to find five or six dependable beta readers.

You want specifics from your betas, not generic "I kind of liked it" sort of comments. To aid in this, editor Jodie Renner suggests fifteen questions to give your betas:

1. Did the story hold your interest from the very beginning? If not, why not?

2. Did you get oriented fairly quickly at the beginning as to whose story it is, and where and when it's taking place? If not, why not?

3. Could you relate to the main character? Did you feel her/his pain or excitement?

4. Did the setting interest you, and did the descriptions seem vivid and real to you?

5. Was there a point at which you felt the story started to lag or you became less than excited about finding out what was going to happen next? Where, exactly?

6. Were there any parts that confused you? Or even frustrated or annoyed you? Which parts, and why?

7. Did you notice any discrepancies or inconsistencies in time sequences, places, character details, or other details?

8. Were the characters believable? Are there any characters you think could be made more interesting or more likable?

9. Did you get confused about who's who in the characters? Were there too many characters to keep track of? Too few? Are any of the names or characters too similar?

10. Did the dialogue keep your interest and sound natural to you? If not, whose dialogue did you think sounded artificial or not like that person would speak?

11. Did you feel there was too much description or exposition? Not enough? Maybe too much dialogue in parts?

12. Was there enough conflict, tension, and intrigue to keep your interest?

13. Was the ending satisfying? Believable?

14. Did you notice any obvious, repeating grammatical, spelling, punctuation or capitalization errors? Examples?

15. Do you think the writing style suits the genre? If not, why not?

Freelance Editors

Good beta readers help you with the overall story. Often, this will be enough. But sometimes you may want to hire what's called a *developmental* editor. This is someone who is experienced in handling big picture issues in your chosen genre.

How do you find such an editor?

Recommendations are best. But you can do research online. There are many freelance editors (sometimes calling themselves "book doctors") who were once part of a traditional publishing house in New York. Downsizing over the last several years has put many of them in the freelance market.

Look at their websites. Look at client lists and endorsements.

Before you hire, ask for a sample edit. One page. You are entitled to know what you're getting for your money.

Not all writers feel the need for a developmental editor, but if you're just starting out, it can be a good investment. Near the start of my career I was fortunate to work with a great developmental editor at the publishing house I'd signed with. He would send multi-page, single-spaced letters critiquing my manuscripts. These were always painful to read, but it was good pain, the kind that made me stronger as a writer.

Once you have a manuscript ready, especially if you are going to publish it yourself, get it to a proofreader. Typos are the bane of the self-publishing writer's existence.

Again, find proofreaders through recommendations or research.

Eventually, you'll find yourself with a team you can trust.

Market Study

A wise pulp writer looks at the market, what's selling, what's popular. And then puts that knowledge together with what he's happiest writing.

Then he adds his own particular style, his voice. That's the spice you add to the genre conventions. It's like the banter in Raymond Chandler, or the musings on society in John D. MacDonald's Travis McGee series.

It's you on the page, filtered through your characters. (I have written a book on **Voice: The Secret Power of Great Writing.**)

Note: happiness in writing can also be like arranged marriage. You can learn to love a new genre as you write. The nice thing about pulp writing is that you can do a story or even a book in a new genre, to see how you like it, and also to see what feedback you get.

TECHNOLOGY

The pulp writers of today have so many advantages their forebears did not enjoy, nor could even conceive. Today we have:

DICTATION

You can speak your text into a dedicated program, or on apps on your phone. Erle Stanley Gardner, back in his day, had a team of secretaries who took down his dictation. He would be quite jealous of us if he only knew.

I use dictation on occasion, though I prefer to type. My prose comes out differently when I speak it. But that's probably because I've spent most of my literary career on a keyboard. But I'm glad the option is there.

SCRIVENER

Many writers, including this one, swear by Scrivener. But just as many writers, I think, have avoided it because, at first blush, it looks "too complicated."

Yes, Scrivener has a lot of bells and whistles. But you don't have to be conversant with them to use the program effectively. You can start simply by using it as brainstorming partner, a corkboard to view your scenes, and an organizer for your manuscript and your research.

If you're interested, I wrote a blog post at *Kill Zone* on how to get started with Scrivener.

SCAPPLE

This is a mind-mapping app created by the same folks who gave us Scrivener. It makes brainstorming easy. I use it for thinking about the big picture, and also for preparing to write scenes. You can do mind-mapping on paper, of course, but I like having the ability to move items around on the screen at will.

EVERNOTE

Another program many writers love is Evernote. It lets you create and organize research notes with lots of ways to collect data (e.g., text, web page, attachments, etc.) You can also import Evernote files into Scrivener.

No doubt there will be many more such apps available in the future. The point is to find and use the ones that are an aid to productivity, and not stress about the rest.

And you may simply choose the old-fashioned way—typing —exclusively.

It's up to you. The only rule for the pulp writer is to keep up the forward motion.

Which brings me to:

. . .

NaNoWriMo

This is National Novel Writing Month, held in November of each year. The heart of a pulp writer should pound with happy anticipation at its approach. The goal is to write a 50,000-word (pulp size!) novel in one month. People all over the world participate. It's a supportive community, and you can find out all about it at their website, nanowrimo.org.

While many—perhaps most—of the writers who take the challenge just wing it (this is called "pantsing," as in flying by the seat of your pants every day), I think there is a better way.

Spend the month of October (in addition to your writing quota) to draft a very simple plan for your novel.

Start by creating what's called an "elevator pitch." That is, a three-sentence squib that gives you the basic, high-concept spine of your story.

Sentence one is character + vocation + current situation.

Sentence two starts with "When" and is what I call the Doorway of No Return—the thing that pushes the Lead into the main plot.

Sentence three begins with "Now" and the death (physical, professional, or psychological/spiritual) stakes. Here's an example based on *The Insider* by Reece Hirsch:

> Will Connelly is an associate at a prestigious San Francisco law firm, handling high level merger negotiations between computer companies.
>
> When Will celebrates by picking up a Russian woman at a club, he finds himself at the mercy of a ring of small-time Russian mobsters with designs on the top-secret NSA computer chip Will's client is developing.
>
> Now, with the Russian mob, the SEC and the Department of Justice all after him, Will has to find a way to save his professional life and his own skin before the wrong people get the technology for mass destruction.

This foundation will keep you on track as you write.

Now, there are many ways to go further in planning your novel. Some writers like to be rather extensive with outlines, others are scared of them, and still others are somewhere in between. For NaNoWriMo try, at the very least, my 3 x 5 card exercise.

I love doing this in the early stages of my own novels. I take a stack of 3 x 5 cards to my local coffee joint and just write down scene ideas. Random. Whatever vivid scene comes to my mind. I might prompt myself by playing the dictionary game (opening a dictionary to a random page, picking a noun, and riffing off that). When I have 30-40 scenes I shuffle the deck and pick two cards at random and see what the connection suggests.

Eventually, I take the best scenes and put them in some sort of rough order.

NaNoWriMo is, at the very least, a great way to up your tempo and production. That's entirely worth it for the pulp writer.

THE TOP PULP GENRES

The golden age of the pulps was also the great era of the mystery. Readers couldn't get enough of them—nor could the movie studios, which often based B pictures on stories plucked from one of the pulp magazines.

Two types of mysteries were featured regularly. The so-called "cozy" type, wherein a somewhat benign sleuth navigates clues in a non-threatening environment to find the murderer. This remains a popular mystery sub-genre.

The other type popular in the golden age was one featuring a hard-boiled detective. To this day that influence is felt. Michael Connelly's Harry Bosch probably wouldn't be around if it hadn't been for Raymond Chandler's Philip Marlowe. Robert B. Parker's Spenser was admittedly in this tradition.

The mystery genre works because crime never goes away. Readers love to see justice done in the pages of fiction.

Note, this category does not have to give us a professional gumshoe. Perry Mason, the lawyer-hero created by Erle Stanley Gardner, was really a detective in disguise, solving mysteries and then engineering a successful courtroom defense. Agatha Christie's

Miss Marple was a kindly old lady who just happened to have tremendous powers of observation.

The basic plot pattern in a mystery is simple.

Somebody is killed (or kidnapped).

The Lead character has a reason to solve the murder. Sometimes it's his job. Other times because it's personal.

The Lead asks a lot of questions, and gets a lot of the runaround. In the hard-boiled genre, he may also get beaten up, or shot.

The Lead eventually solves the case.

Today, this genre is usually placed under the Mystery/Thriller umbrella. While popular, there is one genre that exceeds it —Romance.

According to the 2017 survey of Smashwords authors, romance represented 73% of its top 200 bestselling titles.

So if you're just starting out in pulp, and want to get in on the most profitable segment of the market, you can start with Mystery/Thriller or Romance. Or both! Many a successful author has combined the two, in a genre called Romantic Suspense.

Note, however, that in such a crowded field you need to make your work stand out in some way. The most important consideration here is your characters. (See the next chapter for tips on creating a compelling series character.)

What are the other most popular genres today?

Fantasy
Science Fiction
Young Adult/Teen
Historical
Action/Adventure
Horror

While there is still a small niche market for Westerns, this category does not show up on most lists of bestselling genres. But if you love it, why not try to bring it back? I write the occasional boxing story set in 1950s Los Angeles. That sort of "men's action" was big back then, not so much now. I don't care. I like it. I just don't do it exclusively.

So here is my advice. Either write what you love, or choose a popular genre and *learn* to love it. (Remember my "arranged marriage" analogy? Well, here it is again). When you love what you're writing, your writing will be better, and it needs to be in this era of so much digital content.

When I think of the great pulp writers, I always include Robert E. Howard, creator of Conan the Cimmerian. Those stories would combine Action/Adventure and Fantasy. Howard found his most sustained success with this series character.

But that did not stop him from selling other kinds of stories in horror, detective, boxing, and Westerns. He was a pulp *writer*, and proved it with his wide reach and production, all before his tragic suicide at the age of thirty.

So choose ... write ... experiment ... and when you hit on something that works, hammer out more of it.

Especially if you come up with a great series character.

THE PULP WRITER'S INSURANCE POLICY

"The pulp writer's insurance policy: continuing characters." — Erle Stanley Gardner

PULP FICTION WRITERS OF OLD MADE MUCH BANK WITH A HIT series character.

Sherlock Holmes is the best example of the concept. So popular was Holmes that his creator, Sir Arthur Conan Doyle, couldn't get out from under him. At one point he killed off his detective, but the public demanded he be brought back. His resurrection was by way of the novel *The Hound of the Baskervilles.* When it was first published in *The Strand* magazine, the circulation of that periodical went up by about thirty thousand.

In other words, Doyle, though feeling a bit trapped, took that feeling all the way to the bank.

WHAT MAKES A GREAT SERIES CHARACTER?

I see five qualities in the best series characters. If you can pack these in from the start, your task is half done. Here they are:

1. A point of uniqueness, a quirk or style that sets them apart from everybody else

WHAT IS UNIQUE ABOUT SHERLOCK HOLMES? HE'S MOODY AND excitable. Among the very staid English, that was different.

Jack Reacher? Come on. The guy doesn't own a phone or clothes. He travels around with only a toothbrush. Funny how every place he goes he runs into massive trouble and very bad people.

Writing in First Person POV presents a further opportunity: a unique and memorable voice. This was my choice in a series of pulp-style boxing stories I've written about a character named Irish Jimmy Gallagher. I was inspired to try this by the Sailor Steve Costigan boxing stories of pulp master Robert E. Howard. (A sample story is included in this book. See Appendix 4.)

2. A skill at which they are really, really good

KATNISS EVERDEEN IS KILLER WITH THE BOW AND ARROW.

Harry Potter is one of the great wizards (though he has a lot to learn).

3. A rebel

THE SERIES HERO SHOULD RUB UP AGAINST AUTHORITY, EVEN IF it's in a quiet way, like Miss Marple muttering "Oh, dear" at the local constabulary. Hercule Poirot is a needle in the side of Inspector Japp.

4. A vulnerable spot or character flaw

ROBERT E. HOWARD'S CONAN THE CIMMERIAN HAS A VICIOUS temper that sometimes gets the better of him.

Sherlock Holmes has a drug habit.

Stephanie Plum keeps bouncing between two lovers, who complicate her life.

5. A likable quality

PHILIP MARLOWE HAS SOME OF THE GREATEST QUIPS IN THE history of crime fiction. We like them because Marlowe is also vulnerable—to getting beat up, drugged, or otherwise manhandled by forces larger than himself (like Moose Malloy).

Wit is one of the great likability factors.

Another is caring for others besides oneself. Stephanie Plum has a crazy family to care for, not to mention her sometime partner Lula.

WILL THE CHARACTER GROW?

One decision you need to make early on is how much character growth there will be. While you'll hear a lot about the necessity for character arcs, they aren't always necessary.

For example, Jack Reacher doesn't change. I once heard Lee Child talking about this on a panel, and he said, "Arcs? We don't need no stinkin' arcs."

Ahem.

Michael Connelly, on the other hand, has brought tremendous change to his series character, Harry Bosch. He decided, too, that he would age Bosch right along with the books, a decision he has come to ruefully regret. Bosch is getting up there!

At the very least, your character ought to grow stronger with each adventure. Why? Because without that there is no tension or conflict in the story. Each new tale must challenge the character in some way that threatens him with death (physical, professional, or psychological).

TEST MARKETING

Self-publishing today provides the pulp writer with a way to "test drive" a potential series character. You can do that in a number of ways.

You can write a story and send it to several beta readers. These are people you know and trust to give you honest feedback.

You can publish in a free venue, like Wattpad, and collect the feedback that way.

There's always the option of going to Kindle Direct Publishing and using Kindle Select exclusivity so you can promote the story for free. Promote the heck out of it. Read the reviews.

The pulp writers of old weren't shy about testing a character and then moving on if that character didn't create enough buzz. Their big problem was the lag time between sending in a story and waiting months for it to appear.

Today, you don't have to wait.

GENERATING PLOTS

Pulp is plot.

The characters in pulp serve the plot.

Of course you can go inside a character. Just don't get stuck there.

Readers of pulp fiction want action. *Kiss kiss, bang bang* as the old saying goes.

Thus, the prolific pulp writer spends the majority of his creativity time coming up with ideas for ripping-good stories.

And relies upon certain "formulas." Which is a word often sniffed at by the literati. Allow me to unsniff it.

In *Theme & Strategy* (Writer's Digest Books) Ronald Tobias gets it right:

> We say we prize originality above all else in art. Originality is the artist's brilliance, that indefinable something that is distinctly the artist's and no one else's. What gets lost in all that praise of individuality is that originality is nothing more than seasoning added to stock. Seasoning gives distinct flavor, its character or charm, if you will, and seasoning gives the distinct taste that immediately identifies the dish as unique. But we forget that the

foundation remains the same, and that the chef and the diner both rely on that fact.

A chef's genius is not to create a dish from original ingredients, but to combine standard ingredients in original ways. The diner recognizes the pattern established in the foundation of a baked stuffed turkey, and we look for the variation, the twist that will surprise and delight us. Perhaps it's in the glaze or in the stuffing, something that makes that turkey different from all the other turkeys that came before it.

As you develop an idea for a story, start with the foundation, the pattern of action and reaction that is plot.

In my workshops I'm sometimes asked how to keep plot and structure from devolving into formulaic writing. My answer is similar to what Tobias says above. You don't cook an omelet with a watermelon. If I want an omelet, I want it made with eggs in a pan with some ingredients and spices. What those add-ons are and how they are proportioned make up the distinctiveness—the originality if you will—of the dish.

In the same way, eggs are the basis of the formula. It's what readers expect from a story. They don't want to be confused or frustrated. Of course, an author is free to write experimental fiction, which is also known by its unofficial name, Fiction That Doesn't Sell.

But if you're in this game to make some dough, you'll use familiar ingredients but you'll spice them up with your unique brand of characterization, dialogue, and voice.

The late, great writing teacher Jack Bickham wrote the following in *Scene & Structure* (Writer's Digest Books):

> Mention words such as structure, form, or plot to some fiction writers, and they blanch. Such folks tend to believe that this kind of terminology means writing by some type of ... predetermined format as rigid as a paint-by-numbers portrait.

Nothing could be further from the truth

In reality, a thorough understanding and use of fiction's classic structural patterns frees the writer from having to worry about the wrong things, and allows her to concentrate her Imagination on characters and events rather than on such stuff as transitions and moving characters around, when to begin or open a chapter, whether there ought to be a flashback, and so on. Once you understand structure, many such architectural questions become virtually irrelevant – and structure has nothing to do with "filling in the blocks."

Structure is nothing more than a way of looking at your story material so that it's organized in a way that's both logical and dramatic.

So don't get ensnared by the ruinous idea that formula is the enemy of originality.

Instead, become a great chef. Know your ingredients. Cook up a delicious tale by mixing the familiar with your unique blend of spices.

Your readers will eat it up.

PLOT IDEAS ARE EVERYWHERE

Write down every idea you get, even if it's only one line.

Ideas are everywhere. You should never ask yourself, "How do I find a great plot?" Your question should be: "Which one of my long list of ideas should I develop next?"

Your imagination is a muscle. The more you use it, the stronger it gets. It begins to work on its own. Stephen King called this phenomenon "the boys in the basement."

The boys (or girls if you prefer) get trained the more you ask yourself *What if?*

When you see a billboard: *What if the people in that scene were kidnapped?*

When you see a woman standing on the corner waiting for the light to change: *What if she is a hit-woman out on a job?*

When you're waiting in line for coffee: *What if this guy in front of me has taken on another identity?*

When you see a news item: *What if I twisted that item a little bit? Made the man a woman, or vice versa? Or set it in a small town instead of the city? Hmmm ...*

Write them all down.

Play the first-line game (one of my favorite exercises). Just write some great opening lines. You don't have to know anything about the plot or the characters. Just make it a line that would absolutely grab the lapels of a reader and make them read the next line.

Keep a file of these.

You will have many more ideas than you can get to in your lifetime. This is a comforting thought to the pulpster.

Now you decide which idea you want to develop into a plot.

My own practice is to go through my lists periodically and sense which ones jump out at me. Get me wondering. Have me seeing a potential story.

I put these into a file I call "Front Burner Concepts." I'll then spend half an hour typing a free-form document, talking to myself about the idea. I'll put down potential plot twists, stakes, characters, motivations. A story will begin to take shape.

This is similar to the development process in a movie company. Last of all I'll consider the marketability of the concept. I need to have the following:

A lead character I care about deeply.

A unique spin on plot and setting.

Death stakes.

A cast of colorful supporting characters.

When I green-light a concept, I develop my elevator pitch (as described in the chapter "Conditions for Success." And then I map out my signpost scenes (as explained in my book, *Super Structure*).

Then I give myself a SID—Self-Imposed Deadline.

And I'm off.

THE QUINTESSENTIAL PULP PLOT

In his classic book on fiction craft, *Techniques of the Selling Writer,* the pulp writer turned writing teacher Dwight V. Swain recounts a letter he received from an editor who was "riding herd on a chain of pulp magazines." The editor, one Howard Browne, wanted Swain to provide him with some content. This is what he wrote:

> I've got an assignment for you, keed. I want 25,000 words a month—one story—that is ACTION! The type of yarn, for instance, where a group of people are marooned in, say, a hilltop castle, with a violent storm raging and all the bridges out and the electric power gone and the roof threatening to cave in and corpses falling down stairs and hanging in the attic and boards creaking under somebody's weight in the dark ("Can that be the killer?") and flashes of lightning illuminating the face of the murderer only the sonofabitch is wearing a mask that makes him look even more horrible, and finally the girl has been given into the safekeeping of the only person who is absolutely not the killer —only he turns out to be the killer, but he has taken the girl where no one can get to save her and you damn well know he is raping her while everybody stands around helpless. Do these stories in the style [Edgar Rice] Burroughs used to use; you know, take one set of characters and carry them along for a chapter, putting them at the end of the chapter in such a position that nothing can save them; then take another set of characters, rescue them from their dilemma, carry them to a hell of a problem at the end of the chapter, then switch back to the first set of characters, rescue them from their deadly peril, carry them along to the end of the chapter where, once again, they are seemingly doomed; then rescue the second set of characters ... and so on. Don't give

the reader a chance to breathe; keep him on the edge of his chair all the way through. ... GIVE ME PACE AND BANG BANG! Make me breathless, bud!

There's never been a better—or more entertaining—definition of pulp plotting than this. Absorb the philosophy, and add to it your own settings and characters and themes and inner fire.

Plot. Action. Entertainment.

Make the readers breathless!

FRANK GRUBER'S FOOLPROOF PLOT FORMULA

Frank Gruber, author of *The Pulp Jungle*, had his own plot formula. Here is his checklist:

1. Colorful hero
2. Inside info on the subject matter
E.g., police procedure, or facts about an enterprise, like cock fighting. Readers like to learn things.
3. Villain
Stronger than the Lead
4. Colorful background
Find the unique details
5. Unusual murder method
Can be gun or knife, but used unusually
6. Motive
Only two—hate and greed, with subsets
7. Clue
Key clue must be there for reader to find
8. Trick
When all seems lost, hero gets out with unusual method
9. Action
Not talk, talk, talk
10. Climax

Grand, smashing, unusual

II. Emotion

Hero personally engaged, above and beyond merely being paid.

ERLE STANLEY GARDNER'S PLOTTING PHILOSOPHY

In a book about Erle Stanley Gardner's methods, *Secrets of the World's Bestselling Writer*, Gardner's philosophy is evident. "I served the reading public," he once stated. "The reading public is my master." Thus:

> In my stories I try to figure myself as a prospective buyer of a magazine standing in front of the hotel newsstand. Would my story title make me pick up the magazine to look at it? Would the first hasty glance through the story make me buy the magazine, and would the reading of the yarn make me a regular subscriber? I know it can't be done, not right at the start anyhow, but there's no harm in being ambitious.

In one of Gardner's notebooks he wrote:

Work on every plot until you have:

1. Unusual opening incident
2. Complete character conflicts
3. Some emotional appeal
4. Some unusual slant of characters and situation
5. All stock situations eliminated

Make genuine reader suspense in which she doesn't know what will happen next and is surprised either by (A) what does happen; (B) the way in which it happens.

Here are a few more thoughts from Gardner:

A good plot never hops into a person's mind ... A plot has to be built. ... The public wants stories because it wants to escape. ... The writer is bringing moral strength to many millions of people because the successful story inspires the audience. If a story doesn't inspire an audience in some way, it is no good.

The point is that a writer in starting a story should first decide what lowest common denominator of public interest, or what combination of common denominator he's going to put in the story. Once he puts them in the story he knows he is starting on a firm foundation. If he doesn't have them in the story he doesn't have anything.

People love to dream, people love to yearn.

My definition of a mystery is that it consists of a series of interesting events which have sinister implications and the logic of which cannot be instantly comprehended by the audience. Therefore it seems almost essential to me that we should open our stories with some event which attracts the interest of the audience, which seems to have somewhat sinister overtones because they know they're going to be watching a murder mystery, and which simply intrigues the hell out of the audience.

Lester Dent's Master Fiction Plot

One of the most successful of the pulp writers was Lester Dent (1904-1959). In his relatively short life he churned out at least 175 novels, most of them about the titular character Doc Savage (these books and stories were published under the "house name" Kenneth Robeson).

Dent famously championed a formula for his pulp fiction, and shared it with readers of *Writer's Digest* in 1936. He used the 6,000 word short story as the template. Dent divided up that word count into four sections of 1,500 words each. With a little adjustment, you could apply the same principles to a novella (20k-50k words) or novel (>50k).

FIRST 1500 WORDS

1—First line, or as near thereto as possible, introduce the hero and swat him with a fistful of trouble. Hint at a mystery, a menace or a problem to be solved—something the hero has to cope with.

2—The hero pitches in to cope with his fistful of trouble. (He tries to fathom the mystery, defeat the menace, or solve the problem.)

3—Introduce ALL the other characters as soon as possible. Bring them on in action.

4—Hero's endeavors land him in an actual physical conflict near the end of the first 1500 words.

5—Near the end of first 1500 words, there is a complete surprise twist in the plot development.

SO FAR: Does it have SUSPENSE?

Is there a MENACE to the hero? Does everything happen logically?

At this point, it might help to recall that action should do something besides advance the hero over the scenery. Suppose the hero has learned the dastards of villains have seized somebody named Eloise, who can explain the secret of what is behind all these sinister events. The hero corners villains, they fight, and villains get away. Not so hot.

Hero should accomplish something with his tearing around, if only to rescue Eloise, and surprise! Eloise is a ring-tailed monkey. The hero counts the rings on Eloise's tail, if nothing better comes to mind. They're not real. The rings are painted there. Why?

SECOND 1500 WORDS

1—Shovel more grief onto the hero.

2—Hero, being heroic, struggles, and his struggles lead up to:

3—Another physical conflict.

4—A surprising plot twist to end the 1500 words.

NOW: Does second part have SUSPENSE?

Does the MENACE grow like a black cloud? Is the hero getting it in the neck? Is the second part logical?

DON'T TELL ABOUT IT***Show how the thing looked. This is one of the secrets of writing; never tell the reader—show him. (He trembles, roving eyes, slackened jaw, and such.) MAKE THE READER SEE HIM.

When writing, it helps to get at least one minor surprise to the printed page.

It is reasonable to expect these minor surprises to sort of inveigle the reader into keeping on. They need not be such profound efforts. One method of accomplishing one now and then is to be gently misleading. Hero is examining the murder room. The door behind him begins slowly to open. He does not see it. He conducts his examination blissfully. Door eases open, wider and wider, until—surprise! The glass pane falls out of the big window across the room. It must have fallen slowly, and air blowing into the room caused the door to open. Then what the heck made the pane fall so slowly? More mystery.

Characterizing a story actor consists of giving him some things which make him stick in the reader's mind. TAG HIM.

BUILD YOUR PLOTS SO THAT ACTION CAN BE CONTINUOUS.

THIRD 1500 WORDS

1—Shovel the grief onto the hero.

2—Hero makes some headway, and corners the villain or somebody in:

3—A physical conflict.

4—A surprising plot twist, in which the hero preferably gets it in the neck bad, to end the 1500 words.

DOES: It still have SUSPENSE?
    The MENACE getting blacker? The hero finds himself in a hell of a fix? It all happens logically?

These outlines or master formulas are only something to make you certain of inserting some physical conflict, and some genuine plot twists, with a little suspense and menace thrown in. Without them, there is no pulp story.

These physical conflicts in each part might be DIFFERENT, too. If one fight is with fists, that can take care of the pugilism until the next yarn. Same for poison gas and swords. There may, naturally, be exceptions. A hero with a peculiar punch, or a quick draw, might use it more than once.

The idea is to avoid monotony.

ACTION: Vivid, swift, no words wasted. Create suspense, make the reader see and feel the action.

ATMOSPHERE: Hear, smell, see, feel and taste.

DESCRIPTION: Trees, wind, scenery and water.

THE SECRET OF ALL WRITING IS TO MAKE EVERY WORD COUNT.

FOURTH 1500 WORDS

1—Shovel the difficulties more thickly upon the hero.

2—Get the hero almost buried in his troubles. (Figuratively, the villain has him prisoner and has him framed for a murder rap; the girl is presumably dead, everything is lost, and the DIFFERENT murder method is about to dispose of the suffering protagonist.)

3—The hero extricates himself using HIS OWN SKILL, training or brawn.

4—The mysteries remaining—one big one held over to this point will help grip interest—are cleared up in course of final conflict as hero takes the situation in hand.

5—Final twist, a big surprise, (This can be the villain turning out to be the unexpected person, having the "Treasure" be a dud, etc.)

6—The snapper, the punch line to end it. The suspense held to the last line.

Everything been explained?

It all happen logically?

Is the Punch Line enough to leave the reader with that WARM FEELING?

Did God kill the villain? Or the hero?

[JSB note: The bit about God killing the villain is a warning against *Deus ex machina,* which basically means you can't have some coincidence or "outside agency" killing the bad guy (or solving the major plot problem). It has to be the hero, in some form or fashion, doing the work and "earning" the victory.]

All this should be enough to convince you that plots can be found in abundance. If you're still unsure, then let me suggest my Start-A-Plot Machine in the back of this book.

No more excuses, okay?

TAKING YOUR PULP TO THE NEXT LEVEL

Pulp fiction is action-oriented. Its motto is, *Grab 'em and don't let go.*

As a result, pulp is often charged with being hack work. Meaning that the style is too simple to be considered "literary."

The charge is made among those who think it is a cosmic injustice that popular fiction makes more money than literary fiction (as a general rule).

Mickey Spillane, the hard-boiled paperback king who was once the best-selling author in the world, was always being put down as a hack. One day he took a break from counting his money and said, "Those big shot writers ... could never dig the fact that there are more salted peanuts consumed than caviar."

I happen to like salted peanuts *and* caviar. But when I write pulp fiction, I want the bowl filled with goobers.

Which does not mean you cannot shape those legumes into a pleasing form. That, after all, is what the really great pulp writers did. As I've mentioned earlier, some of the best American writers *period* came out of the pulp era. Raymond Chandler is studied in college classrooms today. His style is inimitable and has stood the test of time.

One of my favorite authors is John D. MacDonald. He wrote a

string of paperbacks in the 1950s that I would place alongside any output of that time. Better than Norman Mailer or James Jones or a whole host of middlebrow writers (the Book-of-the-Month club crowd). His insights into character and his unobtrusively poetic prose set him apart from most of his contemporaries.

Elmore Leonard got his start in the 50s with pulp-style Westerns before moving on to crime paperbacks. He is now considered a master of the fiction craft, especially dialogue.

So there I've mentioned three areas for you to consider if you want to kick your pulp writing up a notch—style, deeper characterization, dialogue. I'll add a fourth: cliché hunting.

STYLE AND CHARACTERIZATION

Chandler used to type his stories on half-sheets of paper. In this way he concentrated on every sentence. While that process may prove to be too slow for most pulp writers, slowing down in certain strategic sections offers you a chance to put some sparkle in your prose.

John D. MacDonald's prose had what he said he strove for, a bit of "unobtrusive poetry." In other words, it was evocative but didn't get in the way of the story. It added to the depth of the tale.

Second, his insight into human nature was broad, so when you got into a character you really got into the push-and-pull of his inner life. While that aspect never takes over the story, it certainly makes it all the more compelling. You want to know how the plot ends, but also how a character's life is going to be changed—for better or for worse?

Your prose style should be intentional—something you are aware of and work on. At minimum, pulp fiction has a straightforward, storytelling function. Isaac Asimov had some thoughts on this in his memoir *I. Asimov*. Reflecting on how to be prolific, he said:

If you try to turn out a prose poem, that takes time, even for an accomplished prose poet like Ray Bradbury or Theodore Sturgeon.

I have deliberately cultivated a very plain style, even a colloquial one, which can be turned out rapidly and with which very little can go wrong.

That is certainly enough to be a pulpster, but you may want to go further. I'm going to give you a technique to make that happen, but I will mention that I've written an entire book on *Voice: The Secret Power of Great Writing,* which is my complete statement on this subject.

My suggestion is that you find places in your story where your character is experiencing emotional pressure. Ideally, a story has that thread running throughout, because if a character doesn't feel pressure, the stakes aren't high enough.

What I mean is to pick a scene and locate the "hot spot" in that scene, the central focus of it. Let's say in your crime thriller your protagonist, Dirk Jones, a PI, has to tell a woman that her husband has been murdered. He goes to the house, there's some hemming and hawing, the woman offers coffee, etc. But then the news must be delivered. The hot spot is like this:

"There's no easy way to put this," Dirk said.

"It's Hank, isn't it?"

Dirk nodded.

Jen put her hand on her mouth. Closed her eyes. A pitiful whimper sounded in her throat.

Dirk said, "You need to sit down."

"Don't tell me that!" Jen turned and ran upstairs.

A door slammed.

Dirk thought for a moment about going after her. But he decided to let it go. She needed time to be alone.

He took a sip of coffee. It was bitter and lukewarm.

Then he put the cup down and left through the front door.

That's fine, and in fact may be just the right tone for you. But let's play with this. Put a mark after the word *lukewarm*. This is the place where we're going to go a little deeper.

Open up a new document. You are going to write a "page-long sentence." This is a run-on, fast-as-you-can-write sentence exploring as much of Dirk's emotional landscape as possible. If you really are feeling it, please don't stop at one page. Keep going. Don't worry about style. Just get the thoughts down, and let them lead you wherever they want to go.

> Yeah, bitter and lukewarm, like my damn life, like it's always been, and Pop told me that's what I was, lukewarm and a coward, afraid to face anybody or anything, so when I left home for the first time at sixteen I made sure I screamed in his face How's this for lukewarm! How's this, Pop! I'm getting out for good! and all he could do was stare at me like I wasn't even his son, like I was an alien or something, and here I am in the middle of this thing, this killing, and my damn soul is as cool as that damn coffee, because I don't really care, I closed off caring, remember when you did that, pal, you were in San Antonio that time, that one time you found somebody who really cared about you, loved you in fact, that's what she said, and you used her for a week then walked out on her and never looked back, so why don't you for once follow up on something and go up there and tell this woman you're not going to walk out on this, you're going to find out who killed Hank, and if you do maybe you'll connect with a person like a real human being is supposed to ...

After you do your own page-long sentence, set it aside for half-an-hour or so, then come back, read it over and highlight the things that jump out at you. You will find good stuff, every time. It may only be one line, but that line will be gold.

Now put that material in your text after the mark.

Try this again in two or three other places, and you'll have both expanded your style and deepened your character.

Your style is expanding, your character work deepening. And this material won't overtake the plot.

DIALOGUE

Pulp writers—especially those who write thrillers, noir, and crime—know that a huge part of the craft is tough talk, dialogue from the mouths of hardboiled protagonists, street hustlers, cops, thugs, hit men, femme fatales, homme fatales, and other denizens of the dark side.

I'll tell you off the bat it's more than just lacing a page with profanities. There are more artful ways to do it.

1. BE WITTY

This isn't always easy, but it pays big when you can pull it off. The master of this kind of gab, of course, was Raymond Chandler. His novels featuring PI Philip Marlowe are filled with snappy banter that works because (and this is the key) it is perfectly in Marlowe's *voice*. It never seems to be a strain. Like this exchange in *The Long Goodbye:*

"See you around," the bodyguard told me coolly. "The name is Chick Agostino. I guess you'll know me."

"Like a dirty newspaper," I said. "Remind me not to step on your face."

Or this from *The Little Sister:*

"That slut. What does she say about me?" she hissed.

"Nothing. Oh, she might have called you a Tijuana hooker in

riding pants. Would you mind?"

The silvery giggle went on for a little while. "Always the wisecrack with you. Is it not so? But you see I did not then know you were a detective. That makes a very big difference."

"Miss Gonzales, you said something about business. What kind of business, if you're not kidding me."

"Would you like to make a great deal of money? A very great deal of money?"

"You mean without getting shot?" I asked.

"Sí," she said thoughtfully. "There is also that to consider. But you are so brave, so big, so—"

"I'll be at my office at nine in the morning, Miss Gonzales. I'll be a lot braver then."

Take your time with exchanges like this. Don't force the issue. Play with the language. A different word here or there can make all the difference. I always liked the line from one of Lawrence Block's Matt Scudder short stories. Two cops are talking about a suspect who is not exactly lovely to look at. One cop asks the other how ugly is this guy? And the other cop says, "God made him as ugly as he could then hit him in the face with a shovel."

2. Be Crisp

Tough talk is often clipped. It gives nice white space to the page, too. This was Robert. B. Parker's preferred method. Here's a bit from one of his Sunny Randall novels, *Melancholy Baby:*

"Sarah took a lot of drugs."

"More than grass?" I said.

"Oh, yes. Hard drugs."

"Like what?"

"I don't know. I don't use drugs."

"Good for you," I said.

"I graduate this June, and next year I want to be in a really good MBA program. I don't want to do anything to spoil my chances."

"So her drug use was disruptive?"

"Yes. She'd come in at night, late sometimes, and act crazy."

"Like?"

"Like she'd be crying and seeing things and ..." Polly shook her head. "Did you ever go to college?"

"I did," I said.

"What did you major in?"

"Art."

"Really?"

I could tell that Polly found that puzzling.

"How did you do?"

"I was a good artist and a bad student," I said.

3. Be Over the Top

This is the opposite of #2. It should be done sparingly. But every now and then consider having one of your characters give vent with a paragraph or two of straight tough talk.

Mickey Spillane liked to do this. He of course invented the quintessential hard-boiled PI, Mike Hammer. But he also wrote stand-alones. In *The Long Wait* (1951) the narrator, Johnny McBride, has been dragged in by the cops for questioning. McBride insults the cops (this will get him beaten up later) and tells them to inform him of the charges or let him walk. The lead detective says:

"I don't know what kind of an angle you think you're playing, McBride, and I don't give a damn. The charge is murder. It's murder five years old and it's the murder of the best friend a guy ever had. It's murder you'll swing for and when you come down through the trap I'm going to be right there in the front row so I can see every twitch you make, and there in the autopsy room when they carve the guts out of you and if nobody claims the

body I'll do it myself and feed you to the pigs at the county farm.
That's what the charge is. Now do you understand it?"

Pick a tense moment of tough talk and put yourself inside one
of the characters. Write a 200-word rant. Do not pause to edit.
Come back to it later and review. Even if you only end up using
one line, it'll be a good one.

Go over all your dialogue scenes and look for words to cut.
Replace some verbal answers with silence or an action beat. You'll
love the results.

4. Be Suggestive

Again, tough talk does not have to be laced with expletives.
You're a writer. You have a whole palette of possibilities open
to you.

Writers of the 40s and 50s often simply wrote things like: *He
cursed and walked out of the room.* You know what? That still works.
Readers can fill in the blanks in their own heads.

There are other methods. In *Romeo's Way*, I have a character,
Leeza, who is young and foul-mouthed. Mike Romeo is trying to
help her. She doesn't want any. This character would definitely
unleash a curse storm. But I didn't want to lay that on the reader.
So I did it this way:

She jumped back like I was the guy from Friday the 13th.
"I don't think you're safe here," I said.
"What the h—"
"No time to talk. Come with me."
I put my hand out. She slapped it. "Get away from me."
"I'm on your side," I said.
She began a tirade then, peppered with words with a hard K
sound. She was a symphony of K. It was so constant and crazy, it
hit my brain like woodpecker woodpecker peck peck woodpecker.

"Ease up," I said. "There's bad people who want you. Did you forget that?"

Woodpecker woodpecker!

"Your boss, one of your bosses, Kat Hogg, is in a car over there. Come with us."

Leeza looked across the street. Then she turned and ran.

I said something that sounded like woodpecker myself and gave chase.

I've written a book on dialogue with the subtitle *The Fastest Way to Improve Any Manuscript.* I do believe that. Any agent or editor will tell you that good, crisp dialogue is a sign the writer knows what he's doing.

While there is a whole lot that can be said on the art and craft of dialogue, let me give you a couple of simple techniques that will deliver big dividends to the pulp writer.

5. CUT ALL YOU CAN

Go through all your dialogue and cut as much of it as you can. Often you'll begin dialogue with fillers—*Look, Well*— or with needless words, which are often *No* and *Yes.*

Consider:

"You want we should go downtown?"
"Yeah, let's go raise some hell."

As opposed to:

"You want we should go downtown?"
"Let's go raise some hell."

Just a little bit crisper. Readers pick up on that.

. . .

6. Use action beats

In addition to cutting the "flab" in your dialogue, think about cutting entire lines and replacing them with action.

Consider:

"You're driving me crazy."

"Get out right now before I do something I regret!"

"I'm going, I'm going!"

As opposed to:

"You're driving me crazy."

She picked up a pen and held it like a knife.

"I'm going, I'm going!"

7. Place information within confrontation

Characters should always talk to each other the way they would in real life. That means they don't simply spout information both already know. That's a cheap way to deliver the info to the reader, and it shows.

Not:

"Come along, Sylvia. We'll be late for the Robinson's and you know how Charlie likes to see you, my wife, because you always laugh at his jokes."

The best way to deliver this kind of stuff is in an argument.

"Come on, we'll be late."

"Who cares?"

"Charlie Robinson, that's who."

"I don't like the way he looks at me."

"Then don't laugh at his jokes."

"Why don't you take a poke at him?"

"Why should I?"
"You're my husband. Act like one."

Cliché Hunting
A cliché is a shortcut, a quick way to get from one moment to the next with the least possible thought. Readers, if they are being entertained, probably don't mind a cliché or two. But if you freshen them up, they will be delighted. And delight helps sell your next book.

You can catch clichés as you write, and change them on the spot. Or, if you're going good, you can wait until you edit.

I like to do a light edit on my previous day's pages, so that's usually when I do it.

Two ways to go.

1. You can dump the whole cliché and replace it with a fresh image.

Suppose your protagonist is feeling extreme anxiety. Maybe you quickly wrote something like: His gut clenched. Or: He was tied up in knots.

Dean Koontz, who began his writing life as a prolific paperback author (with several pseudonyms) has the protagonist in *The Husband* suffering through the kidnapping of his wife. He's alone at home:

> To Mitch, standing on the back porch, this place, which had previously been an island of peace, now seemed as fraught with tension as the webwork of cables supporting a suspension bridge.

2. You can freshen the cliché itself.

Harlan Ellison, in one of his stories, wrote, "She looked like a million bucks tax-free." That little addition tax-free takes it out of the realm of cliché.

What might you do if you found yourself writing, "She was as honest as the day is long."

Maybe: She was as honest as the day is long. Unfortunately, it was nighttime.

She was a diamond in the rough.

Perhaps it would be appropriate to write, "She was a diamond in the buff."

Ahem.

You get the idea.

If you were to give each of these areas a day of attention during the revision process, your pulp will begin an inexorable rise toward the top of the heap. While there's no telling how far that climb will be, it is a virtual guarantee that it will be higher than it would have been had you skipped these steps.

Try it and see.

PUBLISHING STRATEGIES

You've got your pulp story or novella or novel ready for prime time. You've had the piece looked at and edited (refer back to the chapter "Conditions for Success").

What do you do now?

You get it published.

Where?

You have two choices: traditional venues and do-it-yourself.

TRADITIONAL

If you have a full-length novel and want a publishing house to partner with, you'll need to learn how to write a proposal you can submit either to an agent or an editor. This is a subject that I cover fully in *The Art of War for Writers* (Writer's Digest Books). There is also abundant advice available for free on the internet.

Just be aware of a few items:

1. Not all agents are good, and a bad agent is worse than no agent.

2. Publishing contracts are a minefield for the uninformed. So

either get informed or a good agent or a good Intellectual Property lawyer to go over the contract. The clauses you want really want to notice are the Non-Compete and Reversion of Rights. On the former, make sure you aren't prevented from putting out stories or novels on your own if you so desire. On the latter, tie the reversion clause to a minimum of royalty income per every six months. $500 minimum.

3. Your publisher might go out of business.

4. Your cut of the proceeds will be around 25%.

5. You will have to do most of your own marketing.

For shorter pulp works, as of the time of this writing (oh citizens of the future) there are still some print outlets for genre fiction. The most popular are: *Alfred Hitchcock's Mystery Magazine, Ellery Queen Mystery Magazine*, and *Suspense* (mystery, suspense, thriller), *Asimov's Science Fiction*, and *Analog* (science fiction and speculative fiction).

SELF-PUBLISHING

From the start of the digital publishing revolution—which officially began with the introduction of Amazon's Kindle in November, 2007—I wrote that this feels like a new era for pulp fiction. Authors began turning out genre stories and novels and publishing them on Amazon for 99¢.

In other words, abundant and cheap fiction.

What was missing, of course, was the curation of competent editors. The old pulp magazines had literate and savvy publishers, the best of whom could spot and nurture talent. Not so the Amazon marketplace, which was open to all.

Which meant, because of Sturgeon's Law, that the market

would be flooded with crap. Sturgeon's Law holds that 90% of everything is crap. What a good editor tries to do is weed out that 90%.

Those early years of digital self-publishing saw a tsunami of bad writing, bad covers, and bad reviews.

But then ... the cream began to rise.

A writer named Hugh Howey scored big with his series of short sci-fi works. They drew a following. Why? Because they were *good.* That following led to a collection that became *Wool,* a self-publishing sensation.

Other writers began to attract a following, with the pulp formula of fast + quality. Quality being defined as *something readers are glad they read.*

These successful authors wrote novels (50k words or more), novellas (20k +), novelettes (7k +), short stories (1k +). They figured out their own curation system—beta readers, critique partners, freelance editors. They worked.

So when it comes to short pulp works, I recommend self-publishing, and doing so through Amazon's exclusive Kindle Select program. That way you can run promotions that offer your story or novella for free. That way you begin to gather new readers.

For full-length novels, self-publishing is of course available. The question is whether to "go wide" with retailers or to stick with Amazon exclusivity. There is no single right answer to this. Arguments can and will continue to be made on both sides. If you're just starting out, however, your goal is to gain eyeballs. The promotional benefits of Kindle Select (which only bind you for 90 days at a time) might be the way to go. After you've built a readership, you can make the decision whether to expand or not.

The most successful self-publishers, just like the most successful writers from the old pulp days, operate like a business. There are a few key principles to learn, and good practices to engage in. For a full treatment, please see my book *How to Make a Living as a Writer.*

Another form of self-publishing is online serialization. There are sites like Wattpad, which is described as a "free online story-telling community" where you can post short stories and get comments from readers.

There are also serializing sites that offer the chance for the writer to make a little lettuce. One such is Radish. It's a serialized fiction app that enables writers to post stories in bites, build up an audience, and eventually earn money with gripping serials readers want to pay to read. *Publishers Weekly* did a story on Radish, quoting the co-founder Seung-yoon Lee:

> Lee said "the timing is right [for a change in digital reading]. We see a decline in e-readers and as a result a decline in e-book sales."
>
> The key to mobile digital reading, Lee said, is to offer original short genre fiction with 2,000-word chapters, written in a conversational style with cliff hangers.
>
> He even envisions a fiction formatted much like a text message app, a style Radish's young readers are comfortable reading on a phone. "Writing on Radish is a style somewhere between TV screenwriting and novel writing," he said.
>
> Radish, he said, is modeled after such platforms as Wattpad, the Toronto-based online reading and writing community for young consumers who read on smartphones, as well as companies like China's Shanda Literature (2.5 million active writers and 120 million users) or Kakaopage, a Korean serial fiction platform. These sites, he said, offer original short serialized genre fiction written expressly for smartphones. (Lee also notes he has met and conferred with the founders of these platforms.)

Radish generates revenue by selling readers "coins," which are a form of online currency that allows Radish readers to open a new chapter in a serial without waiting for access. Revenue is split 50-50 with the author.

MARKETING YOUR PULP

While this is not a book on the nuts and bolts of self-publishing and promotion, there are a few basics that are simple to learn. You of course need a website. For best practices on setting up a site, have a look at what Jane Friedman has to say:

www.janefriedman.com/author-website-components/

The abundance of material on marketing out there may seem overwhelming. You can quickly develop a case of marketing dysphoria, where you're sure there's always something more you should be doing lest you miss out on the "tipping point" of big sales.

That's bad for you and bad for your writing. And since by far the best marketing is having a good product, you can actually be losing future revenue by taking too much brain power away from improving your craft and spending it on fruitless marketing jags.

In my book *Marketing for Writers Who Hate Marketing*, I simplify the marketing spectrum by emphasizing that you should do a few things well. Those things are:

1. Your writing
2. Your book description copy
3. Your covers
4. Your email list
5. Your pricing

Everything after that is discretionary, to be undertaken as time allows. I can recommend the following as your next steps:

If you're in Kindle Select, you can do a free promotion for five days, every quarter. Plan to get the word out via social media, friends, and a deal-alert email. The most powerful (and thus hardest to break into) deal-alert is BookBub. Take time to study its requirements. There's a lot of valuable information for free on their blog:

insights.bookbub.com

Don't get discouraged by BookBub rejection. It happens most of the time! There are other sites that are more accommodating. Reedsy has a searchable list of these promotional sites, with price ranges and links:

blog.reedsy.com/book-promotion-services

Plan to use these sites on a rotating basis. You'll pay for this and may not make back the cost of the ad, but that's okay. You're investing in future readers. If you give them good product, they'll stick around and buy more of it down the line. So think of every reader as having a lifetime value, not just a one-time return.

CONTESTS

There are numerous contests out there for your pulp—short stories and novels alike. One of the biggest is the International

Thriller Writers Award (ITW is an organization you should join, and membership is free). I had just written and self-published a pulp-style novella, *One More Lie,* when the awards were opened up to short stories. I was honored when *One More Lie* became the first self-pubbed work nominated for this award. A few years later my self-pubbed novel, *Romeo's Way,* won the award in the best e-book original category. I mention these because putting them into the competition was easy to do and the subsequent attention a great boon. You can find all you need to know at their website:

thrillerwriters.org

Writer's Digest magazine has an Annual Popular Fiction Award. This competition spotlights short fiction in many categories including Romance, Thriller, Crime, Horror, Science-Fiction, and Young Adult. It comes with a cash prize, a spotlight about you in one of their issues, and a paid trip to their hugely popular Writer's Digest Conference. Find out more at:

writersdigest.com/writers-digest-competitions

Other contests of interest may be found by simple search. Some of them are connected to conferences, which brings us to:

CONFERENCES

A good writing conference is a great way to network with other writers and industry professionals. You can learn about your craft, about marketing, about best author practices. You'll meet experts who can give you advice on research. You might actually make a friend or two.

Two of the best conferences are Bouchercon and ThrillerFest, both of which I've attended on numerous occasions. I've never failed to come away with new contacts and information that has proven useful.

Don't be shy about this, but also do some prep work. My colleague at the group blog Kill Zone, Laura Benedict, has some sterling advice:

BE CONFIDENT.

This sounds difficult, I know. Sometimes you just have to fake it until you feel it. The NYT bestselling writer waiting in the coffee line ahead of you sits in front of the same blank page that you do every day, thinking, "What comes next?" You have that in common. You're there for a reason, so act like it.

BE PROFESSIONAL.

This is part of your job. Be sure you note the name of the person you're talking to. It's okay to ask, and asking is far preferable to ending up halfway through an impromptu lunch, petrified that you'll be called on to perform introductions if someone else shows up. If small talk is required, talk about a panel or interview you just attended, or a book you recently read. Not your gallbladder, kids, or most recent tooth implant.

BE READY TO LEARN.

Immerse yourself in the conference agenda. People who are interested in the same things you're interested in put the panels and events together. It's not all about networking.

BE CURIOUS.

Most people love to talk about themselves. Ask questions about their work, their pets, their hometown, their (professional) passions. Most wildly successful authors are good at making other people feel special in a short space of time. Really.

BE MODEST.

We've all gotten the FB messages: "Hey, we're friends now. Buy my book!" Every writer wants other people to know about their work. But don't make that your main goal. Your goal is to learn things, make new friends, and reconnect with old friends. There's always a good time to exchange cards or bookmarks or websites. Name-dropping is a bit gauche, but allowed in small doses if it's relevant to the discussion—or makes a better story.

BE GRACIOUS.

Be as nice to the mid-list or self-published writer standing beside you as you are to the editor you would kill to have publish you. Chances are you'll have far more contact with that writer in your career than you will the editor. Not everything is about getting ahead. It's about being a decent human being. Few things are uglier than people who spend their professional lives sucking up and kicking down.

BE GENEROUS.

You didn't get to where you are as a writer all by yourself. I guarantee that someone around you has less experience. Introduce yourself to someone who looks as uncomfortable as you feel. Make them feel special. It won't cost you anything, and the benefits are precious.

BE ON TIME.

Even if you consistently run five minutes late every other day of your life, when you're in a professional situation like a conference, be on time. Schedules can be tight, and people often do things in groups. (But don't fret about sneaking into panels late, or leaving during. Just be discreet.)

BE AVAILABLE.
If you're not Cormac McCarthy, or Emily Dickinson, leave your room! Put on deodorant, brush your teeth, comb your hair, and attend a panel, a cocktail party, or a lecture. Or even go hang out in the bar. You're over twenty-one, and you're allowed. See and be seen. That's the way it works.

JSB'S START-A-PLOT MACHINE

Erle Stanley Gardner, author of the Perry Mason series of stories and books, was at one time the bestselling writer of all time. How did he manage it?

First, by typing a million words a year.

Next, once he got rolling, by dictating his books to a team of secretaries.

And, finally, by never stopping.

Something he did early on was to create a "plot machine" for himself. Interestingly, this was prompted by his use of the book *Plotto*, which was written by one William Wallace Cook (who is mentioned prominently in this book!).

This plot machine was a series of cardboard wheels, each with several one-line "spokes" around a plot development. The nine basic elements were as follows:

1. The act of primary villainy.

2. Motivation for the act of villainy: Villain resorts to crime because of desire for____ ("Note difference between a static and

cumulative motivation. Better wherever possible to start with a departure from a cumulative murder motivation—gradually, inexorably, forced to a murder motivation." - Erle Stanley Gardner.)

3. The villain's cover-up: Having committed the act of villainy, the villain tries to conceal it or escape consequences.

4. Complications which arise during and after the cover-up: In trying to flee, villain is confronted by complications.

5. The hero's contact with the act of villainy: The hero contacts the act of villainy either by chance or by deliberation.

6. Further complications and character conflicts: When conflict has been joined and hero comes in contact with villainy there are certain complicating circumstances which make for character conflicts and story.

7. Suspense through hero's mistakes: The complications become involved with the suspense element.

8. Villain further attempts to escape: Villain feeling net closing about him tries to escape by some further act which points to a more exciting dramatic climax when carried through.

9. Hero sets solution factors in motion or traps villain.

It's important to note that Gardner used this machine as a starting point only. The various spokes were brainstorming items. Once he had a combination, he would begin brainstorming and developing a plot.

In the pages that follow, I give you a simple plot-starter machine. Here's how it works.

There are five headings (e.g., Act of Villainy). Each heading has a numbered list. I tell you how many choices there are per heading. Start with any heading you desire.

Google *random number generator* and you'll get their default.

Put in the number range for the heading. For example, Act of Villainy has 82 possibilities. You put in 1 and 82 as the range, then "spin" the calculator. Go to the corresponding number in the list, and put that item into a separate document.

I just did that and the number came up 30. On the Act of Villainy list, that item is "crime at sea." I write that down.

And so on through the other headings.

Know that these are intended to storm your brain. You take each one, and also the combination of them, and think on paper or screen. Go where the ideas lead you. Write a free-form document, without pausing to edit, on what your imagination is coming up with.

Soon enough a plot will begin to take shape, and then you can begin to shape it yourself.

Or if you're stuck in your writing or planning, use any one of these categories to come up with a random idea that can get you unstuck.

And that is always how the pulp writer wants to roll.

OPENING SETTING

List of 70

1. 24-hour restaurant
2. airport
3. amusement park
4. antique shop
5. apartment
6. aquarium
7. art museum
8. bakery
9. bank
10. bar
11. beach
12. boardwalk
13. bomb shelter
14. bookstore
15. boulevard
16. boutique
17. brothel
18. bus depot

19. casino
20. cathedral
21. cemetery
22. center of town
23. church
24. city college
25. city dump
26. City Hall
27. coffeehouse
28. concert hall
29. convention center
30. courthouse
31. day-care center
32. delicatessen
33. department store
34. fast-food restaurant
35. fire
36. fire station
37. freeway
38. golf course
39. health spa
40. high school
41. home
42. hospital
43. hotel
44. industrial park
45. jail
46. mobile home park
47. movie location
48. nightclub
49. office building
50. park bench
51. parking garage
52. playground

53. post office

54. prison

55. public library

56. real estate development

57. restaurant

58. river

59. safe house

60. shelter for battered women

61. shelter for the homeless

62. shipyard

63. shopping mall

64. stadium

65. sushi bar

66. swimming pool

67. synagogue

68. taxi

69. water treatment plant

70. zoo

ACT OF VILLAIN

List of 82

1. abduction
2. assault
3. air piracy
4. armed robbery
5. arson
6. assassination
7. attack (physical/verbal assault)
8. ax murder
9. baby selling
10. bank robbery
11. bigamy
12. blackmail
13. bomb
14. breaking and entering
15. bribery
16. campus rape
17. car bombing
18. car as weapon (running people down)

19. carjacking

20. car theft

21. cattle rustling

22. child abuse

23. cock fighting

24. computer fraud

25. conspiracy

26. contract murder

27. copycat crime

28. counterfeiting

29. crime of passion

30. crime at sea

31. data rape

32. dog fighting

33. drive-by shooting

34. driving under the influence

35. drug dealing

36. drug trafficking

37. embezzlement

38. espionage

39. extortion

40. flag burning

41. forgery

42. freeway shooting

43. gangland slaying

44. gang war

45. hate crime

46. hijacking

47. hit-and-run

48. hostage held

49. indecent exposure

50. insider trading

51. insurance fraud

52. involuntary manslaughter

53. jury tampering
54. kidnapping
55. mail fraud
56. mass murder
57. mob violence
58. money laundering
59. Neo-Nazi protest
60. obscene phone call
61. perjury
62. police brutality
63. political corruption
64. Ponzi scheme
65. prison riot
66. prostitution
67. purse snatching
68. random shooting
69. rape
70. serial killings
71. sexual harassment
72. state-sponsored terrorism
73. statutory rape
74. tagging (graffiti)
75. tax evasion
76. theft
77. treason
78. vehicular homicide
79. vigilantism
80. violence in school
81. voter fraud
82. white-collar crime

MOTIVE

List of 5

1. Money
2. Power
3. Revenge
4. Sex
5. Fame

HOSTILE MINOR CHARACTERS MAKING COMPLICATIONS FOR HERO

List of 24

1. Relative
2. Friend
3. Alcoholic
4. Cowboy
5. Architect
6. Fighter
7. Health nut
8. Bartender
9. Recluse
10. Florist
11. Cop
12. Hairdresser
13. Gun fanatic
14. Writer
15. Firefighter
16. Animal trainer
17. Dog groomer
18. Nudist

19. Actor
20. Waiter
21. Arsonist
22. Slacker
23. Pothead
24. Blind person

TWISTS

List of 23

1. Somebody is dead you didn't expect.
2. Getting knocked out.
3. Planted bomb.
4. Anonymous text or email.
5. A dark secret revealed.
6. An emotional wound revealed.
7. An ally betrays.
8. A guy with a gun walks in.
9. The road is closed.
10. The bridge is out.
11. You thought it was a man, but it's a woman.
12. You thought it was a woman, but it's a man.
13. You thought he/she was dead, but he/she isn't.
14. Surprise witness.
15. The message didn't go through.
16. Corrupt person is really trustworthy.
17. Trustworthy person is really corrupt.

18. The protagonist finds out he/she is related to another character.

19. Accident.

20. Injury.

21. Something false goes viral.

22. Good news gets bad.

23. Bad news gets worse.

THE ARMBREWSTER MEMOIR

A few years ago I wrote a series of pulp-style posts on the group blog Kill Zone. Written from the POV of a writer named William "Wild Bill" Armbrewster. We see Wild Bill dispensing advice to a young wannabe writer. I even made up a bio for Armbrewster that could very well have been true:

WILLIAM "WILD BILL" ARMBREWSTER was born in 1899 in Cleveland, Ohio. He had a troubled relationship with his father, which led to Armbrewster dropping out of high school and riding the rails as a hobo. He was nabbed by yard bulls in Chicago in 1917 and given a choice: go to jail or join the Army. He chose the Army and saw action in France during World War I, winning the Silver Star.

After the war he took up residence in Los Angeles and got a job driving a delivery van for the Broadway Department Store. At night he worked on stories for the pulp magazines, gathering a trunk full of rejection letters.

In 1923 a chance meeting with Dashiell Hammett in a Hollywood haberdashery led to a lifelong friendship between the two. Hammett asked to see one of Armbrewster's stories, liked it, and personally recommended it to George W. Sutton, editor of *Black Mask*. The story, for which Armbrewster received $15, was "Murder in the Yard." After that Armbrewster became a staple of the pulps and was never out print again. Between 1923 and 1935 he averaged a million words a year.

In 1931 he wrote the first in a series of stories featuring Cliff Hanlon, an ex-boxer working as a troubleshooter for the movie studio Empire Consolidated. In 1941 the first of ten novels featuring Hanlon was released to great acclaim. *Falling Star* was turned into a hit movie in 1943, with George Raft in the role of Hanlon. Eventually Humphrey Bogart, Dick Powell, Paul Newman, and Al Pacino would take a turn playing the legendary tough guy.

Known as the man with the red-hot typewriter, Armbrewster wrote many of his stories at a corner table at Musso & Frank Grill in Hollywood. He was granted this favor by the owners, for reasons that remain mysterious to this day (some Armbrewster scholars believe he rescued the daughter of one of the owners from an attack by a street thug).

Over the course of his career, Armbrewster shared his writing wisdom with young writers, many of whom went on to careers of their own. One of them, Benny Wannabe, in his eulogy at Armbrewster's funeral, said, "He told me what it took to become a real writer. And he bought me my first sandwich in Los Angeles."

For his writing advice, read on.

NOW YOU CAN CALL YOURSELF A WRITER

The afternoon crowd at Musso's was loud and obnoxious, like a haberdasher with a hangnail. I sat in the corner with my typewriter, pounding away at the new story for *Black Mask*. It was fighting me. It was pummeling me into the canvas. I was a bleeding mess. So I gave the business to my martini and cursed the page mocking me from the roller. That's when I noticed the kid.

He was just standing there, holding his hat. He was maybe twenty-two, twenty-three, which made him a kid to me.

"Are you Mr. Armbrewster, the writer?" he said.

"Right now I'm Mr. Armbrewster, the stinker. Who are you?"

"My name's Benny. Benny Wannabe."

"So?"

"May I sit down?"

"If you buy me a drink. See that man over there behind the bar? In the red coat? His name is Joe. Go tell him to make another for Mr. Armbrewster and then you can sit."

The kid romped off like a happy puppy. I looked at my typewriter and tried to make my detective say something witty. But he just sat there, the piker.

The kid came back and set a fresh one before me.

"Now, what can I do for you?" I said.

"Well, I ... I'm a writer. I've read every story you've ever written. I think you're the best. Even better than Hammett and Chandler."

I was starting to like this kid.

"And I just wanted to meet you," he said. "Somebody at the hotel said you like to work here, and so I took a chance and here you are."

"You say you're a writer, eh?"

"That's right."

"What have you written?"

"A short story."

"One short story?"

He smiled, nodded. I took a snort of martini. Then I popped the olive in my mouth, chewed, and scowled.

"Don't call yourself a writer just yet, kid," I said.

"But a writer writes," he said. "So I've been told."

I ripped the sheet I'd been working on out of the typewriter, crumpled it, and tossed it on the pile on the floor. "No," I said. "A writer works."

Benny Wannabe cocked his head, like that dog listening to the gramophone.

"Look, kid, it's fine to want to write. It's a hell of a business, though, and if you want to make any money at this thing, you have to work, and hard. You have to look at it as a craft, not some ethereal vapor dancing through your noggin, and sweat and fight until you figure out how to do it. Then you have to put your stuff out there, get rejected, fight some more and keep on writing and fighting and typing, until you die."

"Gee," Benny said.

I closed my eyes.

"I have my story with me!" The kid fished out some folded pages and handed them to me. I scowled again, then read the first paragraph.

*The wind was a torrent that day, the day of my birth, the day of my
beginning life's sad yet remarkable sojourn, and the trees were golden with
leaves that looked like little pots of gold with rainbows coming out of
them, full of the promise of life and song and the iridescence of possibility.
Suddenly, a shot rang out.*

"I'm going to need another drink," I said.

"Right away!"

When the kid came back I said, "Listen, Benny, do you really
want to be a writer?"

He nodded.

"Not just so you can call yourself one. I mean, so you actually
have a chance to make some lettuce at it. You do want to make
lettuce, don't you?"

"Oh, yes sir. I believe in lettuce."

"Do you have a job, Benny?"

"I'm a writer!"

"Not yet you're not. I mean, do you have any source of
income?"

He shook his head.

"What are you using for dough?"

"My savings. I bought a train ticket, then got a hotel room
down the street. The last of it I used on, um, your drinks."

"You want my advice, Benny?"

"Oh, yes!"

I took a fin out of my pocket and slapped it on the table. "Buy
yourself a train ticket home. Go back and get a job and marry the
girl next door. Run for mayor or dog catcher. Join the Elks. Do
anything but write."

Benny's face fell harder than Max Schmeling in the second
Louis fight. He said nothing, trembled a little, and tears starting
pooling in his eyes.

I looked at him for a long time. Fresh-faced kid, right off a
turnip truck, but with a dream. Sort of like a kid I once knew a

long time ago. Born in Cleveland, dropped out of college to ride the rails and see life, hoping to gather enough material to make himself a real writer, going off to war and coming home and writing for years without a sale, but never stopping because of the hunger for it, the love of it. I could see just a spark of that in the kid's misty lamps.

"Okay," I said. "You'll need a job to keep a roof over your head. Go on over to Al's Market on Sunset, tell him Bill Armbrewster sent you. Only don't embarrass me."

"I won't, sir!"

"Then you agree to meet with me once a week, and write what I tell you to write, for a year. You willing to do that, Benny?"

"Yes, sir!"

"All right then. Now you can call yourself a writer. Take the fin. Go tell Joe we want a couple of egg-salad sandwiches and some soup. And between here and the bar make sure you grow a thick skin."

"Yes, sir!"

I liked it that the kid's enthusiasm was back, but enthusiasm only gets you so far in life. The ones who make it are the ones who can get kicked in the teeth, have all the stuffing knocked out of them, and still get up and come back typing.

If this Benny Wannabe could do that, he'd maybe make a real writer yet.

USE YOUR NOGGIN TO GET LOTS OF IDEAS

The kid came in all freshly scrubbed and smelling of Brylcreem. He had a big stupid smile on his face, like he'd just kissed a cheerleader.

"Well, I'm here, Mr. Armbrewster," he said.

"Don't state the obvious," I said. "You want to be a writer, don't state the obvious. Let the reader figure out things for himself."

I was typing at my usual table at Musso & Frank on Hollywood Boulevard. This was the first "official" meeting between Benny Wannabe, kid writer, and yours truly, William "Wild Bill" Armbrewster, professional scribe.

"Go get me a usual, and a Coke for yourself," I said, handing Benny a fin. I took that time to type out a line for my tough guy, Cliff Hanlon, to say to an embezzling bank president. *"Money may not grow on trees, but it certainly sprouts on your girlfriend's ring finger."*

When Benny got back with the liquid, I said, "Where's your notebook?"

"Notebook?"

"You know, that thing? With pages? To take notes?"

"I don't have one."

I slapped my forehead. "You want to be a writer, don't you?"

"More than anything."

"Then you have to write things down. You've got to observe, and record what you see. Look around the room. Tell me what you observe."

He turned his head like Charlie McCarthy and gave Musso's a quick gander. "People eating," he said.

"Wrong," I said.

He frowned.

"You've got to see more than you see, see?"

He shook his head.

I sighed. "Look over there. See that couple?"

He looked.

"Who are they?" I asked.

"Why, I don't know. I never met them."

"I'll tell you who they are. She's a cigarette girl from the Trocadero. He's a bigshot lawyer from downtown. He's also married. And not to the cigarette girl."

"You know them?" Benny said.

"Never saw 'em before in my life, but that's what I see. And in an hour, I can type a story that'll sell to *Dime Detective*."

"But how?"

I tapped my noggin. "Up here, boy. You've got a muscle between those big pink ears of yours. A brain, with an imagination already included. But you've got to work your imagination, like it was training for a distance race. You've got to run it around the track, every day. Do that, and it'll get stronger."

"Gee."

"Now look at the corner over there. What do you see?"

He looked at the big man with a napkin stuffed in his shirt, giving the business to a steak.

"A big man eating a steak," Benny said.

"Try again."

"But—"

"Try, Benny, try. Look at him. What do you see?"

Little furrows appeared on Benny's forehead. He kept looking. That gave me time to give the business to my martini.

Finally, he said, "Maybe he's a policeman."

"Good, Benny, good! Keep going."

"Going?"

"What kind of cop?"

"A ... big one?"

"Think! Why is here?"

"Because he's hungry?"

"I'm going to need another drink."

"Wait ... let me see ... he's off duty."

"That would explain the suit. But why here, at Musso's?"

"He likes the food?"

"Come on, kid, don't make me despair of life! What's strange about a cop, on a cop's salary, eating a steak at Musso & Frank?"

"It's expensive!"

"Ah ha! And what kind of cop can afford an expensive steak?"

"A cop who ..."

"Come on, you can do it."

"A cop who is ..."

"Yes?"

"Getting money on the side?"

I slapped the table. "That's it! Benny, my lad, you've done it! Now keep that imagination whirling. Where would side money come from?"

"Why, from ... bribes."

"Yes! What else?"

"Um ... gambling?"

"Benny, I think I'm gonna cry. You see what you're doing? You're starting from absolute scratch, and you're thinking up a character and several possible story situations. You know what that's called?"

"What?"

"Making stuff up! And that's all this writing game is, boy. We make stuff up, and we jot down the ideas, and then we pick the best ideas and make a story out of 'em. And we do that over and over and over again, until we die."

"Really?"

"In fact, I take half an hour every week just to let my imagination run free. I make up opening lines without knowing anything else. I write down as many ways as I can think of for people to get murdered. I can look at the front page of a newspaper and come up with five or ten great plot ideas on the spot."

"Wow."

"I write 'em all down, without judging any of them. Only later do I look at the ideas and pick out the most promising ones. I put these in a file for further development. In short, my lad, I am never without something to write."

"Man!"

"Benny, you've become positively monosyllabic. So here's what you do. Run over to Newberry's and get a notebook and some pencils. I want you to spend half an hour every day writing down ideas. I want you to go down to Pershing Square and watch people. Make up situations on a dozen people you see there. Go to Echo Park and the Santa Monica Pier. Look at the people in your rooming house. Each one of 'em is a story waiting to be told. You fill up that notebook and come back here in a week."

"Okay, Mr. Armbrewster!" He stood up. "What are you going to do?"

"Me?" I took the page I was working on out of the typer and set it aside. Then I rolled in a fresh sheet. "I'm going to write about a crooked cop tailing a shyster lawyer who's making time with a cigarette girl."

Benny just stood there, smiling.

"Who deep sixes a kid without a notebook. Now get going!"

WRITE AS IF IT WERE IMPOSSIBLE TO FAIL

I was killing a dame when Benny walked in.

The dame was Gilda Hathaway and she was an icy blonde in the story I was pounding out for *Black Mask*. The killer was her husband, an action Jackson named Mickey Hathaway. He was about to use an ice pick on his wife when Benny said, "Hello, Mr. Armbrewster."

"What? Huh?" I looked up from my Underwood, which was sitting on my usual table at Musso's in Hollywood. "Don't you know better than to interrupt a writer when he's typing?"

"I'm sorry, sir, I thought we had—"

"I don't care what we had! Go get yourself a Coke and let me finish my murder!"

Benny put his head down, but he did what I told him. I liked that about the kid.

Mickey dispatched Gilda, then wiped his fingerprints off the ice pick. He was out of the apartment by the time Benny got back to the table.

"Say, kid," I said, "you've got the hangdog look of a mortician without a stiff. What gives?"

"I do have a stiff," Benny said. "It's that story you told me to write. I just couldn't. I don't know, I froze. I just sat there staring at the paper."

"Welcome to the world of the professional writer, son."

"This is what it's like?"

"A blank page is God's way of telling us how hard it is to be God."

He stared at me like I was the blank page.

"Before you try to write anything," I said, "you've got to get your head right. You've got to get your mind running like Seabiscuit at Pimlico."

Benny took a sip of his Coke, looking more concerned than ever.

I took out a White Owl, bit off the end, fired it up. A matronly woman at the adjoining table gave me a hard look. I made a mental note to put her in my story as another victim of the ice pick killer.

"You've got a will to fail," I said.

"I do not!" Benny said. Good. He had a fighting spirit. He was going to need that if he wanted to make it in this game.

"Cool your radiator, Benny. We all have a will to fail. It's subconscious. It's deep in the memory banks. All of the things we tried to do in our past, and failed at, collect there. All the embarrassments we've suffered, all the people who made fun of us, those experiences pepper our brains. It's human nature. We almost always act in order to *avoid pain*. So rather than try something and possibly fail, we freeze up. Or we choose something easy because we know there's no risk of failure. We don't act boldly."

Benny was silent, but I could tell I was getting through.

"Our job is to fight that will to fail, to give it the boot. You were afraid I'd rip apart your story, so you didn't write it."

Benny paused, frowned, then said, "You're right."

"Of course I'm right. This is Armbrewster you're talking to."

"So what do I do?"

"You really want to know?"

"More than anything!"

"More than a new Packard?"

"Yes!"

"More than a sweet gal to smother you with kisses?"

"I kind of want that," he said. "But only after I'm a successful writer!"

"Just what I wanted to hear, kid. So here's what you must do from now on—write as if it were impossible to fail."

"That's it?"

"*It?* Why, boy, I'm giving you the Promethean fire here! If the gods find out I've told you, I could get lashed to a rock and have my liver pecked out by a predatory bird! Which, by the way, isn't all that different from working with an editor."

"But I can't just write that way, can I?"

"You're not a Presbyterian, are you?"

"Methodist."

"Then you're a free-will being! And as such you are in control of your thoughts. And if you don't control them, they will certainly control you. It takes effort, sure, but so does anything worthwhile. Now, have you ever done anything successfully?"

"Sure."

"Like what?"

"I ran the anchor leg on our state championship relay team in high school."

"Aces! Think about that moment."

"Now?"

"No, in the late spring of 1954. Of course now! Close your eyes and keep 'em closed."

He did as I asked.

"You remember taking the baton?" I said.

"I sure do."

"Remember your adrenal glands firing on all cylinders?"

"Uh-huh."

"How about the roar of the crowd, the feel of the track, the exhilaration of crossing the finish line?"

"Yes!"

"Drink it in!"

"I'm drinking!"

"Keep those eyes closed. Your teammates are around you, slapping you on the back."

"Yes."

"And your best girl is in the stands, watching."

"Judy Parrish! How did you know?"

"This is Armbrewster. Now, you're feeling good, right?"

"Yes."

"You see? You're in control of your thoughts and your thoughts feed your feelings. Now, I want you to see yourself standing in Stanley Rose's bookstore, holding your novel from Scribner's in your hands, as a crowd starts to gather for your reading."

Behind those closed lids, Benny's brain was starting to run. When he smiled, I knew he was ready.

"Open your eyes! Next time you freeze up, remember those good feelings and imagine yourself with the book. Then write *as if it were impossible to fail.*"

"Does it really work?"

"A sweet kid named Dorothea Brande wrote a book called *Wake Up and Live!* and it sold a million copies. It's the only way to stomp that will to fail and write your best stuff."

"Gee. I feel better already."

"Swell! Now get back to your room and start typing."

Springing up, he almost knocked over the table. He did a 50-yard dash out the door.

I sat back, remembering when I felt the way Benny did right now—ready to write like the wind. To write as if I couldn't fail. That got me through a lot of cold nights and dismal days. And now here I was, making a living with the written word, but also realizing I'd been skating on the story I was working on. The encounter with Benny left me with the uneasy feeling I was playing it safe, mailing it in, avoiding risks. That old will to fail can sneak up on you like a jungle viper.

"Phooey!" I said.

I tore out the page I'd just typed, crumpled it, tossed it on the small pile at my feet. Then rolled in a fresh piece of paper.

This time, Gilda had an ice pick of her own.

TROUBLE IS YOUR BUSINESS

Benny Wannabe charged up to my table at Musso's and said, "I did it!"

I took my fingers off the Underwood keys. My normally productive digits weren't doing me any good at the moment. I was stuck on a scene. The smiling mug of my young pupil was good for a break.

"Sit down." I leaned back and reached for a cigar. "Now, what is it you did?"

"Started my story! And it felt great. I told myself I was gonna write great today, just like you told me to. And I did!"

"Nice going, kid. Getting words on paper every day is the golden rule. You have a plot?"

"I sure do!"

"Tell it to me."

"Well, it's about a young man who wants to become a writer and uses all his money to buy a train ticket to Los Angeles."

"And?" I said.

"And what?"

"What happens to him?"

"Um, he gets to Los Angeles, where he meets a famous writer."

"Uh-huh. That famous writer better be handsome, brilliant, and witty."

"Of course!"

"Problem is," I said, "that's not a plot."

"It's not?"

"You're just telling your own story, right?"

"How'd you know?"

"Wild guess," I said. "Listen, all new writers think they have an autobiographical story inside them, and that's a great place to keep it. You, you need a plot."

"But I felt great. You told me I have to write like I couldn't fail."

"That doesn't mean you don't have to learn *how* to write. Write as if it were impossible to fail, then clear your decks and look at what you've done and figure out how to make it better. Or find somebody who knows his stuff to help you along."

"Like you, Mr. Armbrewster?"

"You lucky kid. Now let's get down to basics. What's a plot?"

"It's what the story's about."

I shook my head. "Your Aunt Mabel's flowers is 'about something.' Or some kid coming west. For you to have a plot you've got to have trouble."

"Trouble?"

"Write this down. Trouble is your business. A plot without a trouble is like a Duesenberg without gas. Pretty to look at but going nowhere. Readers read in order to have an extended experience of worrying about what happens to somebody. So make 'em worry."

"How?"

"Get your character up a tree. Throw rocks at him. Have lightning hit the tree and set it on fire. Then get your character down. That's a plot."

"Gee."

"So let's take your young writer. Make him so he's not you."

"How?"

"Make him older or younger. Make him from a town without pity, or a runaway."

Benny took out a little notebook and a pencil and started scribbling. "This is good stuff!"

"You're talking to Armbrewster! Here's another one. Make the character not a man, but a woman."

Benny looked at me, pie-eyed. "But I can't. I'm not one."

"Dammit, boy, you're a writer! There's no *can't* in your vocabulary."

"But somebody told me once you have to write what you know."

"Hooey! Write what you burn with, and then find out what you *need* to know to write it."

"But I've never been a woman."

"And I've never been a gangster or a gumshoe! Is that going to stop me? No! Do some research! Go see a Bette Davis movie. There's one playing at the Chinese called *The Great Lie.* Mary Astor's in it, too. Earn the trust of a waitress and ask her questions. And then learn to listen. Half the problems in this world are because men don't know how to listen to women."

"Then what?"

"She's on a train coming west, right?"

"Right."

"What happens on the train?"

"Um, she has dinner and a good, long sleep."

I stuck the cigar in my maw so I could rub my head with both hands.

"No," I said. "She's in her sleeper when a guy with a gun breaks in and covers her mouth."

"But why?"

"Figure it out! That's your job, kid. Bad stuff happens. Your character fights against the bad stuff, because if she doesn't, she's gonna lose something important, maybe even her own life. That's plot and story and the name of this game all rolled into one. When in doubt, when your fingers are frozen over the keys, just bring in a guy with a gun. I said that to Chandler once, and look at him now."

"Raymond Chandler?"

"No, Homer Chandler the delivery boy. Of course Raymond Chandler!"

"But what if I want to write a quiet story about a character, and how he—I mean, she—becomes a better person."

"Ah, you mean you want to be one of the literary boys?"

"Maybe."

"Doesn't matter. Instead of a guy with a gun, you bring in someone who has a psychological gun. Who has power to crush the spirit."

"Yes!"

"Personally, I prefer the rod. But you get to choose, Benny. Just make sure it's real bad trouble."

"That does it!" Benny said. "I'm making her a woman, and bad stuff's going to happen to her."

"That's the ticket. Now go back to your room and start writing. In the first paragraph I want to see a disturbance."

"A what?"

"Am I speaking Chinese here? A disturbance! I don't want to see a florid description or a character who is sleepwalking through life. I want to know that there's a change or challenge happening to your character right from the jump."

"Like a train wreck maybe?"

"It doesn't have to be big, remember that. It can be anything that's disturbing, from a late-night shadow outside a window to a knock on a hermit's door. It can even be some tense dialogue. Just don't warm up your engines! So get to your typewriter and bring me the first three pages when you're done with 'em."

"This is gold, Mr. Armbrewster, gold! I can't thank—"

"It's all right, Benny—"

"—you enough. I'm so excited I'm going to write to my ma and pa and tell 'em—"

"Good-bye, Benny."

"—what a great and wonderful—"

"Benny!"

"What?"

"If you don't go and start writing now, something disturbing is going to happen to *you*."

"Got it!" He rushed out.

I was looking forward to what the kid was going to show me next. A young writer's enthusiasm, if it's mixed with a desire to grow in the craft, always pleases me.

I went back to the scene I was stuck on. Where was I going to go? And then I found myself typing: *A guy with a gun walked in.*

THE FICTION FACTORY

In 1912, a little book called *The Fiction Factory* came out. The subtitle was: *Being the Experience of a Writer Who, for Twenty-Two Years, Has Kept a Story-Mill Grinding Successfully.*

It was by a man named William Wallace Cook using the pseudonym John Milton Edwards. (You can access the entire public-domain book at Gutenberg.org)

EXCERPTS FROM THE FICTION FACTORY

This book is Cook's no-nonsense account of becoming a successful pulp writer through discipline and hard work. His mind and his typing fingers were, to him, a factory, producing product for the various publications open to him.

Jack London advises authors not to wait for inspiration but to "go after it with a club." Bravo! It is not intended, of course, to lay violent hands on the Happy Idea or to knock it over with a bludgeon. Mr. London realizes that, nine times out of ten, Happy Ideas are drawn toward industry as iron filings toward a magnet. The real secret lies in making a start, even though it promises to get you nowhere, and inspiration will take care of itself.

There's a lot of "fiddle-faddle" wrapped up in that word "inspiration." It is the last resort of the lazy writer, of the man who would rather sit and dream than be up and doing. If the majority of writers who depend upon fiction for a livelihood were to wait for the spirit of inspiration to move them, the sheriff would happen along and tack a notice on the front door – while the writers were still waiting.

Cook-Edwards developed a process for himself that produced a certain joy, which was crucial for keeping the fiction factory in full operation. Writing in third-person POV, he states:

> More and more Edwards' experience, and the experience of others which has come under his observation, convinces him that inspiration is only another name for industry. When he was paymaster for the firm of contractors, he went to the office at 8 o'clock in the morning, took half an hour for luncheon at noon, and left for home at half-past 5. When he broke away from office routine, he promised himself that he would give as much, or more, of his time to his Fiction Factory.
>
> What he feared was that ideas would fail to come, and that he would pass the time sitting idly at his typewriter. In actual practice, he found it almost uncanny how the blank white sheet he had run into his machine invited ideas to cover it. After five, ten or fifteen minutes of following false leads, he at last hit upon the right scent and was off at a run. With every leap his enthusiasm grew upon him. A bright bit of dialogue would evoke a chuckle, a touch of pathos would bring a tear, an unexpected incident shooting suddenly out of the tangled threads would fill him with rapture, and for the logical but unexpected climax he reserved a mood like Caesar's, returning from the wars and celebrating a triumph.
>
> In the ardor of his work he forgot the flight of time. He balked at leaving his typewriter for a meal and went to bed only when drowsiness interfered with his flow of thought.
>
> Whether he was writing a Five-Cent Library, a serial story or a novel which he hoped would bring him fame and fortune, the same delight filled him whenever he achieved a point which he knew to be worthwhile. And whenever such a point is achieved, my writer friend, there is something that rises in your soul and tells you of it in words that never lie.

The ideal state of the pulp writer Cook-Edwards described this way:

> The main thing is to break the shackles of laziness and begin our labors; then, after that, to forget that we are laboring in the sheer joy of creation with which our labor inspires us.

Cook-Edwards made a steady income writing pulp novels which, a hundred years ago, were called "nickel novels." They were the precursors to the mass market paperbacks of the 1950s. Cheaply printed, fast to read.

Of course, the literati looked down upon these "dreadfuls" as an affront to art. Cook/Edwards had no patience for this snobbery. He had this to say about the "ethics" of the nickel novel:

> Is the nickel novel easy to write? The writer who has never attempted one is quite apt to think that it is. There are hundreds of writers, the Would-be-Goods, making less than a thousand a year, who would throw up their hands in horror at the very thought of debasing their art by contriving at "sensational" five-cent fiction. So far from "debasing their art," as a matter of fact they could not lift it to the high plane of the nickel novel if they tried. Of these Would-be-Goods more anon—to use an expression of the ante-bellum romancers. Suffice to state, in this place, writers of recognized standing, and even ministers, have written—and some now are writing—these quick-moving stories. There's a knack about it, and the knack is not easy to acquire. No less a person than Mr. Richard Duffy, formerly editor of Ainslee's and later of the Cavalier, a man of rare gifts as a writer, once told Edwards that the nickel novel was beyond his powers.
>
> So far as Edwards is concerned, he gave the best that was in him to the half-dime "dreadfuls," and he made nothing dreadful of them after all. He has written hundreds, and there is not a line in

any one of them which he would not gladly have his own son read. In fact, his ethical standard, to which every story must measure up, was expressed in this mental question as he worked: "If I had a boy would I willingly put this before him?" If the answer was No, the incident, the paragraph, the sentence or the word was eliminated. In 1910 Edwards wrote his last nickel novel, turning his back deliberately on three thousand dollars a year (they were paying him $60 each for them then), not because they were "debasing his art" but because he could make more money at other writing—for when one is forty-four he must get on as fast as he can.

The libraries, as they were written by Edwards, were typed on paper 8-1/2" by 13", the marginal stops so placed that a typewritten line approximated the same line when printed. Eighty of these sheets completed a story, and five pages were regularly allowed to each chapter. Thus there were always sixteen chapters in every story.

First it is necessary to submit titles, and scenes for illustration. Selecting an appropriate title is an art in itself. Alliteration is all right, if used sparingly, and novel effects that do not defy the canons of good taste should be sought after. The title, too, should go hand in hand with the picture that illustrates the story. This picture, by the way, has demands of its own. In the better class of nickel novels firearms and other deadly weapons are tabooed. The picture must be unusual and it must be exciting, but its suggested morality must be high.

The ideas for illustrations all go to the artist days or even weeks in advance of the stories themselves. It is the writer's business to lay out this prospective work intelligently, so that he may weave around it a group of logical stories.

Usually the novels are written in sets of three; that is, throughout such a series the same principal characters are used, and three different groups of incidents are covered. In this way, while each story is complete in itself, it is possible to combine the series and preserve the effect of a single story from beginning to end. These sets are so combined, as a matter of fact, and sold for ten cents.

Each chapter closes with a "curtain." In other words, the chapter works the action up to an interesting point, similar to a serial "leave-off," and drops a quick curtain. Skill is important here. The publishers of this class of fiction will not endure inconsistency for a moment. The stories appeal to a clientele keen to detect the improbable and to treat it with contempt.

Good, snappy dialogue is favored, but it must be dialogue that moves the story along. An apt retort has no excuse in the yarn unless it really belongs there. A multitude of incidents—none of them hackneyed—is a prime requisite. Complexity of plot invites censure—and usually secures it. The plot must be simple, but it must be striking.

One author failed because he had his hero-detective strain his massive intellect through 20,000 words merely to recover $100 that had been purloined from an old lady's handbag. If the author had made it a million dollars stolen from a lady like Mrs. Hetty Green, probably his labor would have been crowned with success. These five-cent heroes are in no sense small potatoes. They may court perils galore and rub elbows with death, now and then, for nothing at all, but certainly never for the mere bagatelle of $100.

The hero does not drink. He does not swear. Very often he will not smoke. He is a chivalrous gentleman, ever a friend of the weak and deserving. He accomplishes all this with a ready good nature that has nothing of the goody-good in its make-up. The hero does not smoke because, being an athlete, he must keep in constant training in order to master his many difficulties. For the same reason he will not drink. As for swearing, it is a useless pastime and very common; besides, it betrays excitement, and the hero is never excited.

The old-style yellow-back hero was given to massacres. He slew his enemies valiantly by brigades. Not so the modern hero of the five-cent novel. Rarely, in the stories, does any one cross the divide. And whenever the villain is hurt, he is quite apt to recover, thank the hero for hurting him—and become his sworn friend. The story must be clean, and while it must necessarily be exciting, it must yet leave the reader's mind with a net profit in all the manly virtues. Is this easy?

Please note this extract from a letter written by Harte & Perkins Dec. 25, 1902—it covers a point whose humor, Edwards thought, drew the sting of dishonesty:

"Your last story, No. 285, opened well, had plenty of good incidents and was interesting, but there are several points in which it might have been improved.

Your description of Two Spot's scheme of posing Dutchy as a petrified boy is amusing, but the plan was dishonest and a piece of trickery. It was all right, perhaps, to let the boys go ahead without the knowledge of the Hero, but when he learned of it he should have put a stop to the plan immediately. It was all right to have him laugh at it, but at the same time he should have spoken severely to the boys about it and ordered them to return the money they had received through their trick. He did not do this in your story and it was necessary for me to alter it considerably in the first part on that account.

The Hero is supposed to be the soul of honor, and in your story he is posed as a party to a deception practiced on the citizens of Ouray, by which they were defrauded of the money they paid for admission to see the supposed "petrified boy." Such conduct on his part would soon lose for him the admiration of the readers of the weekly, as it places him on a moral level, almost, with the robbers whom he is bringing to justice."

Consider that, you Would-be-Goods, who are not above putting worse things in your "high-class" work. And can you say "I am holier than thou" to the conscientious writer who turns out his 20,000 or 25,000 words a week along these ethical lines? Handsome is as handsome does!

Somebody is going to write these stories. There is a demand for them. The writer who can set hand to such fiction, who meets his moral responsibilities unflinchingly, is doing a splendid work for Young America.

WRITING RESOURCES

Here are a few resources for you to continue your writing journey.

First, please take a moment to sign up for my occasional email updates. You'll be the first to know about my book releases and special deals. My emails are short and I won't stuff your mailbox, and you can certainly unsubscribe at any time. In return, you get a free book! CHECK IT OUT.

Online Course

Writing a Novel They Can't Put Down

A comprehensive training course in the craft of bestselling fiction. An investment that will pay off for your entire career.

The books below are by me unless otherwise indicated:

. . .

Plot & Structure

Write Your Novel From the Middle

Plot & Structure

Super Structure

Conflict & Suspense

Revision

Revision & Self-Editing

27 Fiction Writing Blunders - And How Not to Make Them

Self-Editing for Fiction Writers (Renni Browne and Dave King)

Dialogue

How to Write Dazzling Dialogue

Style

Voice: The Secret Power of Great Writing

Description (Monica Wood)(print only)

Publishing & Career

How to Make a Living as a Writer

Marketing For Writers Who Hate Marketing

The Art of War for Writers

How to Write Short Stories and Use Them to Further Your Writing Career

Self-Publishing Attack!

Writing & the Writing Life

Just Write: Creating Unforgettable Fiction and a Rewarding Writing Life Kindle Edition

The Mental Game of Writing
Writing Fiction for All You're Worth
Fiction Attack!
How to Achieve Your Goals and Dreams
How to Manage the Time of Your Life

Nonfiction

On Writing Well (William Zinsser)
Damn! Why Didn't I Write That? (Marc McCutcheon)

Recommended Writing Blogs

KillZoneblog.com
WriterUnboxed.com
WritersHelpingWriters.net
HelpingWritersBecomeAuthors.com
TheCreativePenn.com

ABOUT THE AUTHOR

James Scott Bell is a winner of the International Thriller Writers Award, the Christy Award for Suspense, and many bestselling novels, including the Mike Romeo thriller series. He served as fiction columnist for Writer's Digest magazine and had written several books on the craft of fiction, including the #1 bestselling *Plot & Structure*. A graduate of the USC law school, he lives and writes in the greatest pulp city of all time, Los Angeles.

Made in United States
North Haven, CT
05 May 2024

52153008R00068